Trade Secrets from a Three-Star Chef

Trade Secrets from a Three-Star Chef

TWENTY FOOLPROOF MENUS AND THE SECRETS OF HOW TO PREPARE THEM

Anne Matthews and Nancy Hooper

DOUBLEDAY
NEW YORK LONDON TORONTO SYDNEY AUCKLAND

PUBLISHED BY DOUBLEDAY
a division of Bantam Doubleday Dell Publishing Group, Inc.
1540 Broadway, New York, New York 10036

DOUBLEDAY and the portrayal of an anchor with a dolphin
are trademarks of Doubleday,
a division of Bantam Doubleday Dell Publishing Group, Inc.

Portions of the article by Andy Birsh that appeared in *Gourmet* magazine,
February 1993, are used with his permission.

Library of Congress Cataloging-in-Publication Data

Matthews, Anne (Anne B.)
    Trade secrets from a three-star chef : twenty foolproof menus and the
secrets of how to prepare them / Anne Matthews and Nancy Hooper. — 1st
ed.
        p.   cm.
    1. Cookery, International.   2. Menus.   I. Hooper, Anne.
II. Title.
TX725.A1M383   1994
641.59—dc20   93-25594
                                                                       CIP

ISBN 0-385-42614-3
Book Design by Gretchen Achilles
Copyright © 1994 by Anne Matthews and Nancy Hooper

First Edition

1   2   3   4   5   6   7   8   9   10

To Jeanne Harrison and Bayard Hooper

ACKNOWLEDGMENTS

We wish to thank the following individuals:

Naomi and Irving Fields, Judith Kern, and recipe testers
Lindsay Claire, Linda Hacker, Jayne Peterson, and
Lynne Welch.

Contents

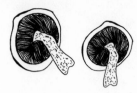

Trade Secrets from a Three-Star Chef

Who Are We...And Why Are We Here?

*M*y introduction to Anne Matthews came as a student in one of her famous wintertime cooking courses. From the moment I entered, I knew this was going to be no Betty Crocker Bake-off; my fellow students were all women—and men—of a certain age, who had clearly come to hone already-established culinary skills for the upcoming Hamptons social season. We considered ourselves serious cooks, and we were happy to pay for the privilege of attending Anne's private cooking school, becoming peers within her "inner circle." All of us had been frequent patrons of The Station at Water Mill, Anne's elegant jewel box of a restaurant.

She had literally taken an abandoned railroad station and transformed it into an intimate hideaway of French Provincial perfection with hunter green walls and a domed terra cotta ceiling, antique Quimper faience nestled in recessed wooden cupboards, fresh flowers, candles, and glowing copper chafing dishes everywhere. Tucked away in a corner was a cozy little back-lit bar, where Anne's partner, Jeanne Harrison, stood ready to concoct world-class martinis for world-weary patrons.

The Station could accommodate no more than forty customers at a time, so to keep the overflow of guests content, Anne and Jeanne installed an old railroad bar car to serve as a cocktail lounge and waiting room. Everything about the place felt authentic, especially when, at least once an evening, the Long Island Railroad clattered noisily along the tracks in the back yard.

Classes were held at the restaurant and were generally preceded by a generous lubrication of Chardonnay or Merlot to take the chill off the winter evening. But as soon as the demonstration began, it was clear that we were in the presence of, well, a formidable presence. Anne is opinionated—about rival restaurateurs, about greedy landlords, about food critics, about the idiocy of American cuisine in general. At times, her flights of vituperation were an art form in themselves, and it soon became apparent that from her many visits to France and her sixteen years as a master chef in Continental and even Chinese cuisine, she had formed a firm and pithy philosophy of cooking. Many of her views will be found in this book, which highlights her work as head chef at the famed Hedges House in East Hampton; as owner and restaurateur of Chinam in Southold; as creator of and chef at The Station at Water Mill; and as a private caterer and chef on Long Island and at her winter retreat in Naples, Florida. To prepare you in advance, here's a sample of her beliefs:

> —The European way of eating—which emphasizes a proper progression of courses from the most substantial to the lightest—may be the only hope for Americans who've eaten themselves sick.
>
> —The pasta craze in this country is insane, and anybody who pays $12.95 for a plate of linguine deserves to be ripped off.
>
> —Good riddance to nouvelle cuisine; it's time we got back to serving food that looks and tastes like what it is.
>
> —Anyone who is *serious* about cooking will own a food processor (preferably a Cuisinart); at least one good, *sharp* knife; and a large, inexpensive, nonstick sauté pan. Moreover, the serious cook will always use sweet (unsalted) butter as well as extra-virgin olive oil (unless otherwise instructed).

TRADE SECRETS FROM A THREE-STAR CHEF

—Almost anyone who can read can cook. Exceptions: food phobics/diet fanatics, hypochondriacs, the mean-spirited, and the miserly.

As week after week she prepared and served one after another of many of the recipes this volume describes, she made converts of us all. But for me, an even more important epiphany unfolded as I watched and scribbled notes. All my life I had wondered how the chefs in first-class restaurants could possibly apply the subtle flavors and elegant details to *dozens* of different meals in such short order, when creating a simple dinner party for eight or twelve often left me exhausted. The answer, which is the true essence of Anne's genius and of this book, lies in the multitude of tricks and shortcuts and even sleights of hand that the professional chef develops over time. Some of the tips may surprise you: Did you know, for example, that the best "fresh" tomato soup starts with canned tomatoes? That you can make an *authentic* Hollandaise sauce in your blender? Expect the unexpected from *Trade Secrets from a Three-Star Chef.*

While working on this book, I've learned more about cooking and food than I ever thought possible. I've added new culinary skills to my repertoire, developed more self-confidence in the kitchen, and discovered that I'm happiest when working at the art of cooking, whether for fun or for profit. It's been a great adventure, and I'm grateful to have had Anne Matthews as my guide.

Nancy Hooper

For years, my restaurant patrons have been trying to con me out of recipes by telling me I'm a genius and I owe it to Western civilization to record my insights for posterity.

I agree with them, of course, but you know how it is with us geniuses—brilliant beyond question, but temperamental; burning with a hard gemlike flame one day, indolent and slothful the next; innovative without a doubt, but inattentive to detail; never wrong, of course, but perhaps a wee bit stubborn and disorganized. To commit my life's work to cold type and precise measurements? Would Mozart write a manual on composing symphonies?

So the concept languished until, one day, Nancy Hooper showed up for my master classes. From the first moment it was clear that, already an accomplished cook, she also had that God-given, intuitive feel for cuisine that transforms cooking from a chore to an art form. Over the months as we got to know each other better, it also became clear that she loved cooking, and even baking, for the sheer joy of it—when I asked whether I could pay her to create some specialty breads for the restaurant, she insisted on producing her beautiful rosemary foccacia and French sourdough bread for free. And when I invited her to join me on a number of catering jobs, she jumped at the chance but never asked, "How much?" (Eventually, she accepted money, but spent it on advertising for Matthews & Hooper: Magicians of the Table, our little fledgling business.)

Soon it emerged in conversation that in her real life she was a published author. Suddenly my prize pupil seemed bathed in an unearthly light. And I realized, as the Zen philosophers say, that coincidence is God's way of remaining anonymous. The two of us set to work to produce our magnum opus.

Later, another miracle revealed itself—not only was Nancy a cook and an author, she had once been an English teacher. This meant that she knew every trick in the book for overcoming sloth, indolence, and procrastination among potential geniuses. For months she held my feet to the fire, refusing to accept vague generalities, demanding specifics—and then going home to test them herself.

I learned to dread the evening phone calls:

"This isn't working. Let's go over the ingredients." Then she would patiently take me through the recipe.

"The butter," I would say lamely. "Did I forget to mention the butter? You must fold in 6 tablespoons first."

"That *would* make a difference," she'd reply coolly.

And so, week by week, month by month, until the book was complete, I humbly learned that genius takes many forms.

Anne Matthews

TRADE SECRETS FROM A THREE-STAR CHEF

1

Achieving Perfection in Four Easy Courses

WHY THE AMERICAN WAY OF EATING IS ALL WRONG

A ll too often in this country, diners start a meal with several double Scotches or martinis, then gorge themselves with watery and gas-producing salads (laden, of course, with high-calorie dressings), plus two or three rolls slathered with butter. Then comes a 16-ounce steak served with a microwaved baked potato stuffed with butter, sour cream, and freeze-dried chives, plus a generous helping of overcooked green beans. The beverage? Inexpensive red table wine. Top all this off with a gigantic piece of apple pie *à la mode* and—*voilà!*—you wonder why you feel ill! In contrast, a European-inspired meal leaves us feeling well fed, wisely fed, and happy.

We suspect it is the dream of every host and hostess to prepare and serve a meal so spectacular, so utterly perfect in every detail, that by evening's end one's guests would rise en masse in a standing ovation. (And, of course, we envision them spending the next several days gossiping among themselves, wondering how in hell we pulled it off!)

If you've ever wanted to stage such a fantasy and bring it to life, this chapter's menu contains the stuff of which culinary dreams are made. The secret lies not so much in the ingredients (though they are quite wonderful), but rather in the harmony

Saucisson Lyonnaise

Breast of Chicken Olivado with Carrot Fritters

Butterflied Pears with Goat Cheese and Butcher-Cracked Pepper

Fine Cognac au Sucre

SERVES 4–6

that is created among the courses: They are served in the European manner—in a specific, gastronomically logical order that makes every sit-down meal an occasion. If you've never tried serving food this way, you are in for an eye-opening experience—and we'll wager that it may change the way you eat forever.

What exactly is the order of courses that creates so perfect a meal? Many opinions abound, but we're partial to Brillat-Savarin's maxim that "the proper progression of courses in a dinner is from the most substantial to the lightest."* How logical this is! Think about it: Instead of relying on the usual heavy, American-style entrée to carry the meal, we start with a genuine appetizer, which assuages our hunger while it also awakens our palates to prospects yet to come. At the second course—usually a relatively small portion of meat plus a vegetable—a sort of miracle occurs: Guests eat slowly and deliberately; they appreciate the subtleties of the meal, and savor every bite. At this point, everyone is happily satisfied but still looking forward to the third course—a sweet finale to be enjoyed quietly, like a reverie; it is this last touch that reminds us the meal is about to come to a close.

These things in mind, let's take a look at our menu:

We begin with the French classic, Saucisson Lyonnaise, chunks of mellow kielbasa and perfectly done potatoes tossed in a delicate vinaigrette. We'll serve small portions. A little will go a long way.

Our second course will appeal to your guests' newly heightened awareness, because it's as gorgeous to look at as it is to eat: the bright yellow of lemon slices and the splendid orange of Carrot Fritters create the perfect accents for the centerpiece—a delicately seasoned, honey-brown chicken cutlet. Pour only one more glass of wine, then sit back and enjoy the scene: Your guests are wondering, what could possibly top this?

The answer: a delightful surprise—an unusual third course of Butterflied Pears teamed with goat cheese and sprinkled with

*Jean Anthelme Brillat-Savarin, *The Physiology of Taste.* Translated by M. F. K. Fisher. New York: Alfred A. Knopf, 1971, p. 4.

TRADE SECRETS FROM A THREE-STAR CHEF

cracked pepper. At this moment, your guests will surmise that you have indeed saved the best for last. But in fact, we're not quite ready to conclude this repast.

Now for the coup de grace: one ounce of cognac for each guest, to be sipped through a sugar cube (instructions to follow). It's hard to imagine a more elegant or unusual finishing touch.

Your guests will be enchanted and impressed by your sophistication, not to mention your ability to serve delicious food in a unique way. But don't overlook these additional benefits of the European order of presentation. It will:

—Encourage healthy eating. The substantial-to-light sequence is a real boon to digestion, not to mention one's sense of well-being. When you serve food in the European tradition, you also eat less food and usually consume fewer carbohydrates and saturated fats.

—Drastically cut the cost of giving a dinner party. Over the course of the meal, you'll be serving far less food than you would ordinarily. And your guests won't care much whether you're serving chicken or a costly leg of lamb: they'll be completely satisfied throughout the evening.

—Enhance the communal pleasure of dining. When food is served this way, the diners spend more time at the table and with each other. They also come away feeling they've had more than a good meal; they feel they were really entertained, by the meal and by each other's company. No wonder European hosts encourage us to have a wonderful time! It goes without saying that we'll have a nice dinner.

Ready? Let's begin. As always, read the recipes carefully a couple of times to make sure you understand the procedures.

NOTE: *We once served this menu for a private party of twenty guests. It doesn't take a rocket scientist to figure out how to increase the ingredients.*

HOW TO TRANSFORM THE TYPICAL AMERICAN MEAL?

It's as simple (and sensible) as changing the order of things, reducing portion size, and eliminating or altering certain ingredients. Here's a shorthand version of how we'd revise the typical "meat and potatoes" menu discussed at the beginning of the chapter:

Spirits: No hard liquor before dinner. Open a lovely bottle of Beaujolais; this light and fruity wine will go with the entire meal.

First course: One half of a baked potato, dressed up any way you wish—e.g., twice-baked with sour cream and real chives, etc.—but *never* baked in foil unless you want a soggy, steamed potato that tastes tinny.

Second course: A 6-ounce grilled sirloin steak (or filet mignon) and a fresh green vegetable.

Third: Salad of your choice (in this menu, we'd serve a vinaigrette dressing rather than a cream-based dressing).

Fourth: A slice of apple pie; if homemade, you do not need any garnishment; if store-bought, you may add a dollop of ice cream.

Saucisson Lyonnaise

In small portions, this is a wonderful first course. If you're lucky enough to have leftovers, you can also serve the Saucisson as a main course for a luncheon: simply add a handful or two of fresh green beans (cleaned, of course, and with ends snipped off) and toss, adding more vinaigrette if necessary.

8	small (or 6 medium) red bliss potatoes
One	16-ounce kielbasa
1/2	tablespoon Dijon mustard
2	tablespoons red wine vinegar
1/2	tablespoon dry vermouth
1/2	tablespoon chicken stock
1/2	cup plus 1 tablespoon extra-virgin olive oil
1	shallot, peeled and finely chopped
1/2	cup finely chopped curly parsley

Into a 2 1/2-quart pot place well-washed but unpeeled potatoes; cover with cold water, cover the pot, bring to a boil, and cook approximately 20 minutes, until fork-tender. Remove the potatoes from the water and let cool.

In the same pot but with newly added cold water, place the kielbasa; bring to a boil, cook for 15 minutes, and remove. When the kielbasa has cooled enough to handle, remove the skin by slicing through the entire length of the kielbasa with a sharp knife; with your hands, carefully ease off the skin. Set the kielbasa aside.

Put the mustard into a small bowl. Whisk in the vinegar, vermouth, and stock. Continue whisking while slowly adding the olive oil. Set aside.

Slice the cooled potatoes and kielbasa into bite-sized rounds and put them in a large serving bowl. Add the chopped shallot and parsley and toss. (Don't be afraid to use your hands.)

(Continued)

WHY START THE KIELBASA AND POTATOES IN *COLD* WATER?

Two reasons: (1) Cold tap water is purer (and therefore tastes better) than hot tap water, which contains sediment from your hot water tank; and (2) if you plunge kielbasa or potatoes into boiling water, the shock may well split their skins.

Rewhisk the vinaigrette and pour half of it over the ingredients. Toss together gently but thoroughly and add more vinaigrette if necessary—a little at a time. Cover with plastic wrap and set aside until serving. *Do not refrigerate.*

Serve on unchilled salad-size plates. To be truly French, serve with Cornichon pickles (available at specialty food markets), a dollop of Dijon mustard, and a freshly baked baguette.

NOTE: *It is not necessary to serve butter with the baguette; instead, dip it into the vinaigrette.*

Breast of Chicken Olivado

The beauty of this dish is that it's light and delicate, yet the small amount of breading gives it the body necessary for a second course. Because the recipe calls for a fair amount of seasoning, don't put salt and pepper shakers on the table.

1/2	cup flour, seasoned with 1 teaspoon salt and 1 teaspoon pepper
4	eggs, well whisked
1 1/2	cups unflavored bread crumbs, preferably homemade
4–6	chicken cutlets, pounded thin
1/2	cup extra-virgin olive oil
2	lemons, sliced into six wedges each
Optional:	1 bunch watercress, thoroughly washed, with tough stems removed

In assembly-line fashion, set out the flour, eggs, and crumbs on separate plates. Then, one at a time, dip the cutlets into the flour and shake off the excess; dip into the eggs, allowing the excess to drip off; then dip into the breadcrumbs, completely covering both sides.

Place the oil in a 12-inch sauté pan and heat to 350°. When the oil begins to sizzle, add the cutlets (do not crowd) and cook approximately 3 minutes on each side, or until honey-brown in color. NOTE: Turn the heat down if the oil begins to smoke. Remove the cutlets from the pan and place them on paper toweling to drain.

To serve, place the cutlets on warmed individual dinner-size plates. Garnish with two wedges of lemon. If you wish, place a small bunch of watercress on each plate.

VARIATION: For a wonderful "Paillard of Veal," pound veal cutlets until thin. Then simply add 1/4 cup grated Parmesan cheese (the real thing, please!) to the bread crumbs and follow the steps above.

TOIL WITH THE BEST OIL...

...and that means "extra-virgin" olive oil. Because it is the purest of all the olive oils—it's cold-pressed, and therefore hasn't been heated or treated with chemicals or preservatives—it is the most flavorful, not to mention the best for you. Don't bother buying a large gallon tank of olive oil—the quality is inconsistent, it turns rancid quickly, and it's loaded with chemicals. You just can't economize on certain things, and this is one of them.

TIP: *Want to reuse cooking oils? Here's a way to do it that works perfectly and doesn't require cheesecloth: Pour the oil through a coffee filter, then store it in a tightly covered jar at room temperature. (Because coffee filters are so dense, this process may take up to 20 minutes; so just pour in the oil and let it sit while you do other things.)*

When you use the oil again (only one more time, please), sauté or fry the same type of food—i.e., oil from this recipe would be used again only for chicken.

A CHOPSTICK WILL MAKE YOU A BETTER COOK

Never again will you serve soggy, greasy sautéed food—if you use a chopstick to determine when the oil is hot enough to seal in the juices of your meat or fish. After the oil has been heating (on medium-high) in a pan for a few minutes, place the tip of a chopstick (the end of a wooden spoon works fine, too) into the oil. When the oil bubbles around the edges of the chopstick, it's at the perfect temperature (about 365°) for sautéing.

SECRETS ABOUT SERVING SIZE

Have you ever felt unsure about how much food to serve for a given course? There's no magic formula, really, but here are some things to think about:

Too much food is defeating to your guests: they're embarrassed not to eat it all, so they do (and then can't eat a bite of the *next* course, which defeats you, the chef). Not enough food can be just as unnerving, but at least your guests will have the option of asking for seconds. (Of course, this assumes you're no longer serving nouvelle food paintings of squash flowers and scallion fronds and nothing to eat.)

Our advice? Take into account your guests and their eating habits. Be mindful of the size of the plate, knowing that an appetizer looks lost and rather silly on a dinner-size plate, but perfect on a salad plate. Then, simply be prudent, and when in doubt, underwhelm rather than overdo. If someone asks for a few more bites, they're complimenting you, the chef. As you become more accustomed to serving meals in the European tradition, you'll become more comfortable with the notion that "somewhat less is more" when it comes to food.

Carrot Fritters

It may take a moment for your guests to figure out what these delicious little "pancakes" are made of. Place them alongside each serving of Chicken Olivado.

8–10	*medium-sized carrots, peeled and cut into 1-inch rounds*
4	*tablespoons flour*
1	*tablespoon sugar*
2	*eggs*
3	*tablespoons sweet butter*

Into a Cuisinart fitted with the steel blade, put the carrot rounds and pulse until grated. Caution: Be careful not to puree them. Place the grated carrots in a medium-sized mixing bowl.

Add the flour, sugar, and eggs and mix together thoroughly. Set aside.

Place the butter in a 12-inch sauté pan and heat to bubbling. With your hands (or a tablespoon), measure out walnut-size dollops of carrot mixture into the frothy butter, pressing down to make each one into a small pancake. Do not crowd them. Sauté 2–3 minutes on each side, until golden brown.

Serve immediately.

Butterflied Pears with Goat Cheese and Butcher-Cracked Pepper

A most unexpected combination of ingredients. Both the cracked pepper and the tanginess of the goat cheese enhance the mellow flavor of the pears.

4   ripe pears, preferably Anjou; washed and cored but not peeled

2   small logs goat cheese (Montrachet is a good name)

Freshly ground pepper

Cut the pears in half lengthwise and slice each half into 6 equal sections. Divide the slices equally among 4 dessert plates, arranging them in a fan-type pattern.

Place 1–2 small rounds of goat cheese alongside each pear, grind on freshly grated black pepper, and serve immediately. To be very French, please serve this dessert with a salad fork and knife.

TRADE SECRETS FROM A THREE-STAR CHEF

Fine Cognac au Sucre

*T*o enjoy this glorious finale, dip one end of the sugar cube into the cognac, then sip the cognac through the cube and repeat the process. Magnifique!

1   ounce fine cognac per person

1   large sugar cube per person

Use small brandy snifters if you have them, or red wine glasses. Pour one ounce of cognac into each glass, and serve on a salad plate lined with a doily or small napkin. (We do this because it's attractive, and it also muffles the sound of the glass hitting the plate.)

Place a sugar cube alongside the base of the glass and serve.

White   Burgundy   Bordeaux   Champagne

WINEGLASS ETIQUETTE

It's fun to serve different wines throughout a meal, but the *way* you serve them is crucial if you want to be utterly correct in the culinary sense.

COMMUNING WITH THE SPIRITS

This is not a menu for non-drinkers, but it is not a menu for heavy drinkers either. We believe one should savor wine with one's food—not use it as an anesthetic! We recommend you serve only two glasses of wine with the entire meal. For fun, try serving two different wines: perhaps a Beaujolais with the Saucisson, then a chilled Chardonnay with the chicken. NOTE: Make sure you use the proper wineglasses!

If you feel you must serve a predinner cocktail, offer each guest one glass of decent champagne. To complaints of being denied hard liquor, simply explain that tonight's dinner is *very French* and that our tastebuds must remain pristine so that we can enjoy every single morsel. *À vos amours!*

DO-AHEAD MISCELLANY

—You may cook the potatoes and sausage early in the day, and mix the vinaigrette. Keep it covered at room temperature until you're ready to assemble the ingredients.

—Pound the chicken cutlets early in the day; keep them in a plastic bag in the refrigerator.

—Pulse the carrots into a coarse grate in advance if you wish; keep them sealed in a plastic bag and refrigerated until ready to use.

—Remember to remove the goat cheese from the refrigerator at least two hours before serving.

NOTE: *The items on this menu do not freeze well.*

MENU-PLANNING PRIMER

Novice cooks tend to plan dinner menus using an equation passed on to them by their mothers: 1 meat + 1 starch + 1 green vegetable + dessert = good dinner. Not a bad combination if you put them in the proper order. But what about the other key elements, such as color, texture, and taste? There's nothing more boring or unappetizing than a bland, beige meal, or one that can be appreciated only by the toothless. So, as you plan your menu, think it through on several different levels.

Example: we know that browns and beiges dominate the Saucisson, so we liven it up with a sprig of fresh parsley. It's relatively soft, too, so we add shallots to the sausage and potatoes for a little crunch, and crisp up the chicken with breadcrumbs. Sautéed chicken cutlet is brownish, so it needs a boost of color, too—we chose lemon slices (tangy) and orange Carrot Fritters (sweet). We accentuate the pale pears (sweet) and white goat cheese (savory) with a sprinkling of cracked black pepper (spicy). In the first two courses, we do a lot of chewing; that's why we follow them with the perfect contrast: melt-in-the-mouth ripe pears and soft cheese perked with pepper.

RULE OF THUMB: *Use your imagination and try to create a sensual dining experience. But don't spend an eternity fiddling with each and every aspect of a menu or you won't have time left for the real joys—cooking the meal, and enjoying friends and family*

2

Reinterpreting the Classics

YOU CAN AND YOU SHOULD!

*O*ne way to scare most home cooks is to take away their cookbooks and urge them to "invent" their own recipes or, at the very least, to reinterpret the classics. Actually, it's easy and fun to create your own version of a classic, and you don't have to have a degree from Le Cordon Bleu to achieve fabulous results.

In this chapter, we'll show you how to defy tradition by changing a few ingredients and by using techniques that, when mastered, can be applied to a variety of dishes. What you learn in the next few pages about Navarin of Shank of Lamb, for example, can help you turn out an unforgettable (and classical) Ossobucco as well. You'll also find plenty of trade secrets, including "do-ahead" tips that make entertaining a breeze.

Start with Anne's brief reminiscence; by way of example, it may give you the courage to experiment on your own. Or simply proceed, undaunted, to the recipes—we guarantee they are "no-fail."

"Most cooks, unless they're gifted with the ability to block the horrors of the past, can remember vividly their most nightmarish moments in or near the kitchen. One of mine occurred ten years ago at a country inn in East Hampton where I first began my career as a professional chef. No, I did not just walk in the door and announce that my great culinary skills would put the place on the map. But I did become the head chef quite by accident—and literally overnight.

"At first, I didn't work anywhere near the kitchen. In fact, when I applied for a job there, the last thing on my mind was cooking. Recently divorced, I simply needed to be employed. The inn's owners were looking for a hostess/bartender, and I got the job on the spot.

"Since I was working the nonfood side of the business, I never gave much thought to the fact that we were serving everything *en brochette* or as shish kabobs, though I must say I thought it comical that here in the midst of the ultrachic Hamptons, an American inn was serving Middle Eastern food—and even impaling it on sticks.

"Unfortunately, an 'eminent' food critic of the *New York Times* found our food anything but amusing. She blasted the restaurant all over the place and that spelled disaster for us. The owners were devastated, most of our customers disappeared, and the moment of truth was at hand.

"'Why don't you put me in the kitchen?' I said whimsically to the owner (who by then had become a friend who'd tasted my home cooking at dinner parties).

"'Why not?' he replied.

"And right then and there, for the first time in my life, at the age of forty-seven, I entered a commercial kitchen to play chef.

"Nervous? I cannot begin to tell you how terrified I was. But who wouldn't be: the restaurant seated 175 and my kitchen crew consisted of a handful of non-English-speaking transients who blew into town on a rickety old potato truck *when* they could get it started. Whether or not they would actually show up to help was the least of my worries. What in God's name was I going to serve?

"Within hours, I'd combed through all my cookbooks, copying recipes by the great chefs of France. The next day, I began practicing my craft on a small, unsuspecting group of customers. Over time, I got rid of meals that didn't move; others I kept and refined to suit my tastes.

"Often, to keep customers interested in coming back again

and again, I would 'reinvent' dishes—I'd start with a recipe from a classical cuisine, but change an ingredient to make the dish new and special. In fact, the restaurant's lack of cash regularly forced me to recreate certain dishes by using cheaper cuts of meat. One of my favorites then as now was an original masterpiece I call Navarin of Shank of Lamb with Spring Vegetables.

"As you will see in the recipe that follows, this dish is really a reinterpretation of the classical French braised lamb stew known as Navarin Printaniere.* But my recipe elevates the lowly *shank* of lamb and transforms it into an elegant yet inexpensive delight. This dish is so good, many of my customers planned their visits to coincide with its offering on the menu."

We think you'll find the menu built around the Navarin uncomplicated but completely satisfying. And please note that you will be serving the salad as a *second* course, to cleanse the palate and prepare it for dessert.

NOTE: *Don't serve wine with a salad course that contains vinegar: the double-dose of acidity ruins the taste of both salad and wine.*

---

*Navarin comes from the navet (turnip), which was once the main vegetable used in the classic dish. Printaniere refers to "spring-like" vegetables.

If you have avoided serving lamb because you feared guests would complain of its "lamby" taste, you need to know about the importance of sugar in certain lamb recipes. Used judiciously, as in the recipe above, a little bit of sugar will eliminate the much-maligned lamby flavor.

As far as we know, no chemical reaction takes place to cause this transformation; perhaps the sugar merely gives the tastebuds something else to contemplate.

Navarin of Shank of Lamb with Spring Vegetables

Try this when you long for something cozy, homey, and deliciously French!

PREHEAT THE OVEN TO 450°.

6	*lamb shanks*
1	*tablespoon sugar*
3	*tablespoons flour*
Two	*13 3/4-ounce cans College Inn beef broth*
One	*13 3/4-ounce can water*
One	*6-ounce can Hunt's tomato paste*
1	*tablespoon chopped fresh garlic*
1	*tablespoon* herbes de Provence *(see page 63)*
1	*tablespoon ground black pepper*
4	*carrots, peeled, cut into 1/2" rounds, and steamed until done to your liking*
One	*10-ounce package frozen baby peas*
6	*large potatoes, peeled and boiled until fork tender*
6	*tablespoons chopped parsley*

Brown the shanks in a 12-inch sauté pan; do not crowd them. Transfer them to a roasting pan large enough to accommodate them comfortably. Sprinkle on the sugar, then place in the oven, uncovered, for a full 5 minutes.

Remove from the oven and sprinkle flour on the shanks. Put back into the oven, still uncovered, for another 5 full minutes.

While the flour is coating the lamb, take the sauté pan you used for browning the shanks and wipe it clean of fat. Then add to the pan the beef stock and water, the tomato paste, garlic, herbs, and pepper. Bring to a *slow* boil, making sure the tomato paste has fully blended into the stock. Remove the shanks from the oven and pour the sauce over them. Cover the roasting pan securely, lower the oven temperature to 350°F, and cook for two hours.

When done, remove the shanks from the roasting pan and pour the sauce into a container, preferably a fat-skimming measuring cup. When cool enough, pour off or remove the fat, which will have come to the surface.

When you're ready to serve, place the shanks in a sauté pan, pour in the sauce, carrots, peas, and potatoes, and *slowly* heat until heated through completely.

Serve each person one shank, one potato, several carrots, and several spoonfuls of peas, and cover *modestly* with the sauce. Sprinkle with parsley and serve immediately.

PLATTER OR PLATES?

Because this menu creates perfect portions, you can and should serve the Navarin on individual warmed plates, not on a family-style platter. No one we know of ever wants to eat more than one shank, so there's no need to have "seconds" available.

You can be heating the Navarin during cocktail hour. Ten minutes before your scheduled seating time, arrange the shanks on individual plates, then ask your guests to come to the kitchen to retrieve their own (or have someone help deliver the plates to the table).

Once you're all seated, that's it: everyone has what's needed, there are no requests for more food, and after dinner there are no messy platters to clear.

TIP: It's insane to serve plates blazing hot. Simply "unchill" them by placing them for 5 minutes in an oven set on low.

DON'T LET YOUR REFRIGERATOR DESTROY YOUR DINNER

Food, like wine, needs to breathe; excessive cold constricts it and sometimes shrinks it. Refrigeration also imparts an "ice-box taste." Common sense tells you that you shouldn't place food in a sun-lit window so that it does a slow bake. But almost any *precooked* dish will do nicely sitting (covered) on your kitchen counter for several hours. Kept at room temperature, your precooked food will taste better when it's finished off later in the day.

Of course, there are exceptions to this rule; they'll appear in other chapters where appropriate. For this menu, however, you needn't refrigerate anything except the lettuce for the salad, if you've prepared it in advance.

Ossobucco

As you will see, this recipe is prepared much like the Navarin, except you'll be deglazing the sauté pan with dry vermouth, and you'll add to the recipe a simple "mirepoix" of sautéed vegetables. As you probably know, any true Ossobucco worth its marrow uses veal shanks *instead of lamb.*

PREHEAT THE OVEN TO 350°.

1	cup flour
	Salt and pepper
6	veal shanks*
2	tablespoons extra-virgin olive oil
1/2	cup dry vermouth
Two	13 3/4-ounce cans College Inn beef broth
One	13 3/4-ounce can water
One	6-ounce can Hunt's tomato paste
1	tablespoon chopped fresh garlic
1	tablespoon dried thyme
6	sprigs fresh parsley

For the mirepoix:

1/2	cup diced celery
1	cup diced carrot
1/2	cup diced onion
2	tablespoons sweet butter

Liberally season the flour with salt and pepper. (Since veal is relatively tasteless, extra seasoning is recommended to bring out

*Ask your butcher for "veal shanks for Ossobucco," cut into 2-inch pieces; do not accept prepackaged skimpy pieces of veal shank—they're uneven in size and weight and won't hold up to the braising technique.

TRADE SECRETS FROM A THREE-STAR CHEF

the flavor.) Then dust the shanks lightly with seasoned flour and shake off the excess.

Brown the shanks on both sides in the olive oil, then transfer them to a roasting pan.

To the same sauté pan, with the fire on high, add the vermouth and heat until it boils. Splash this "deglazing" liquid over the shanks in the roasting pan.

In a separate pan, prepare the mirepoix. Slowly cook the vegetables in the butter until translucent and tender. Set aside.

TIP: Dice all the vegetables the same size; they'll cook evenly and will have the same amount of doneness.

Then, add the broth and water, tomato paste, garlic, and thyme to the mirepoix and blend. Heat slowly until the mixture reaches a simmer. Pour it over the shanks in the roasting pan. Cover the pan tightly and place in the oven for 1 hour and 30 minutes.

Serve the shanks on separate plates, covered with a small amount of sauce and garnished with parsley.

SERVING TIP: Marrow is considered by many to be a delicacy. For a lovely and professional-looking presentation, insert a cocktail fork into the marrow of the center bone. The fork should be standing straight up.

COOKING WITH DRY VERMOUTH

Have you ever noticed that when you prepare a dish that calls for white wine, the resulting taste is often acidic or just plain disappointing? Here's a guaranteed cure for the problem: *Always* use a good dry vermouth in recipes calling for white wine. A high-quality vermouth such as Tribuno Extra Dry produces a lovely finish without acidity, and it's less expensive than a good wine. **Warning:** Never use *sweet* vermouth in place of wine in cooking. A cloying, sweet-sour taste will result.

SPEAKING OF SOUP STOCK

Do not be afraid or ashamed to use canned beef broth in your recipes. College Inn brand is excellent, and has a low sodium content. Important: To eliminate the "tinny" taste of canned beef stock, always add water. For College Inn, use a ratio of two stock to one water. If you're using Campbell's (higher in salt than College Inn), use a ratio of 1 1/2 cups water to 1 cup broth.

Alas, no one has yet come up with a satisfactory substitute for real, homemade chicken stock. But it's so easy to make (and can be frozen) that we don't know why more cooks don't do it themselves. Here's how:

BASIC CHICKEN STOCK

Put 3 pounds of chicken backs and necks in a large stock pot. Add 10 cups of cold water, one peeled and cut-up carrot, a handful of celery leaves, 6 peppercorns, two whole cloves, and one scrubbed but unpeeled sweet potato. (The sweet potato will add richness and a subtle sweetness to any soup recipe.) Simmer on low heat for at least 3 hours. Cool, then skim off the accumulated fat. Freeze in 1-cup plastic containers.

Romaine Salad Vinaigrette

ℋere's a salad that's the perfect foil to the rest of the items on the menu. It supplies a delightful crunch, and the dressing imparts a tangy flavor that is perfect for romaine. Don't forget: This is a second-*course salad—absolutely proper and appropriate in its sequence, though it may surprise or confuse American guests who have a penchant for salad as a first course. Be brave; it's your dinner party.*

2	tablespoons red wine vinegar
1	teaspoon Dijon mustard
1/2	teaspoon Aromat
6 1/4	tablespoons extra-virgin olive oil
2	medium-size heads of romaine lettuce, washed, torn into bite-size pieces, and spun completely dry

Place the vinegar in a jar with a lid; add the mustard and Aromat. Shake until blended. Then add the olive oil and shake again. Pour over the prepared romaine and toss with your hands, thoroughly but with a light touch. Serve immediately.

NOTE: *Do not add salt to the dressing either in the kitchen or at the table. You may, of course, use pepper if you wish.*

SALAD DO-AHEAD TIP

Yes, you *can* do the most laborious prep work for a salad in advance. After following the steps for preparing the lettuce in the recipe, including the spin drying, place the romaine pieces in a salad bowl and store in the refrigerator *uncovered.* (Lettuce wilts only when it's wet; plastic wrap will cause your greens to "sweat.") To avoid serving an "ice-cold" salad with virtually no taste, remove the salad bowl from the refrigerator one hour *before* you plan to serve it. Toss with the dressing just before serving.

WHAT'S AROMAT?

Aromat, made by Knorr (in the yellow container only), is a high-quality mixture of spices that works exceedingly well with any vinaigrette dressing. While it adds tang and body, it must be used *sparingly,* or it will overpower the salad greens!

Aromat does contain MSG, but it won't kill you! Honest! When used judiciously, it does *not* cause headaches or indigestion.

—The Navarin and the
Ossobucco may be pre-
pared in the morning.
Keep covered at room tem-
perature; reheat slowly
before serving.

—Any vinaigrette dressing
can be made days ahead.
As for prepping greens, see
"Salad Do-Ahead Tip" on
page 25.

—You may make your
chocolate cake early in the
day. Just be sure it cools
completely on a rack, then
seal it in a large plastic bag
and keep at room tempera-
ture.

NOTE: *The items on this
menu do not freeze well.*

Chocolate Cake

*Nobody ever believes this recipe came from the label on a can
of cocoa. But everybody loves it, with or without a topping.* (NOTE:
The cake is only one *layer, but it provides ample portions for 6
people.*)

PREHEAT THE OVEN TO 350°.

1	cup cake flour
3/4	cup plus 2 tablespoons sugar
3/8	cup unsweetened cocoa (Ghirardelli is a good brand to use)
1/2	teaspoon baking powder
1/2	teaspoon baking soda
1/4	teaspoon salt
1/2	cup sweet butter, softened
3/8	cup milk
1/4	cup water
1	egg
1	teaspoon vanilla

Grease and lightly flour a 9-inch cake pan or a "mini"
Bundt-type pan (approximately 4 1/2-cup capacity).

Mix all the dry ingredients in a large bowl until well incorporated. Add the liquids in the order given and, with an electric
mixer, beat for about 4 minutes.

Pour into the prepared cake pan and bake in the preheated
oven for 20–25 minutes, or until toothpick inserted in the center
comes out clean. Cool on a rack and serve plain (lightly dusted
with confectioner's sugar), or with ice cream, whipped cream, or
your favorite chocolate frosting.

3

The Ultimate Hamptons Luncheon

FEEDING THE RICH, THE FAMOUS, THE DIFFICULT

If you've never visited the Hamptons, you could be forgiven for thinking they are all of a piece. Certainly from the air they look that way—a fringe of golden sand edging an endless blanket of emerald lawns and stately trees, punctuated by tennis courts, turquoise pools, and expansive dwellings. And the residents are all alike, aren't they? Well, yes and no. One thing they all have in common is that they love giving, or being invited to, weekend luncheons. But the style of entertaining varies widely from town to town.

When the affair is in Southampton, you will probably find your destination just a long 3-iron from the ocean, a stone's throw from the Meadow Club's thirty-six grass tennis courts, and well hidden behind a century-old privet hedge. At the end of the Belgian brick driveway you'll discover not a house exactly, but a structure that may resemble a miniature French château. Most of the trees have a lineage that rivals the guests', and most of the guests have been summering in Southampton for three generations.

When the white-jacketed servant escorts you to the terrace, which overlooks the shimmering sea, you will find, along with the Bloody Marys and chilled Chardonnay, a selection of post-

Prohibition cocktails—Manhattans, daiquiris, whiskey sours. Here and there you will doubtless spot an elegant gent in white flannels, resembling C. Aubrey Smith, contentedly quaffing an ice-cold, bone-dry straight-up martini from a wide-mouthed crystal glass.

An hour later, the now slightly pie-eyed guests will be escorted to the atrium, where something of an anticlimax usually awaits. Perhaps something like deviled eggs, celery stuffed with cream cheese, well-done eggs, well-done bacon, and crisp tan toast with jam—to be washed down with iced white wine or perhaps champagne. The idyll will continue until perhaps 4 P.M., when the party will disperse, only to reassemble a few minutes later at the Southampton Bathing Corporation for—what else?—early cocktails.

Travel five miles down the highway to Bridgehampton, and a quite different ambience awaits. Here the mood is artier, and the effect tends to be rural, with split-rail fences, restored farm-houses, a meadow rather than a lawn, sea grasses and cattails around a pond offsetting the more formal beds of impatiens and day lilies. John and David, the interior designers, have the style down pat, beginning with the postcard invitation dashed off on a pen and ink rendering of their home. It reads, "It would be just super if you guys could come to brunch on Sunday. One-ish. Casual."

Inside the beam-ceilinged, stucco-walled house with wide-boarded original floors, you'll find lots of chintz and an impressive collection of Staffordshire that makes you wish you'd tucked a slingshot into your clutchbag. Luncheon begins with a Danish Mary—served with aqua vit instead of vodka—or a chilled glass of Perrier, no ice, plenty of fresh lemon. Soon, drinks will be upstaged by gorgeous food, everything shipped in from Manhattan's finest food boutiques—Balducci's and Zabar's and Grace's and Artichoke on Sixty-eighth. There's chilled melon soup, served (in a melon half, of course) on china designed by one of the guests. Next, a profusion of smoked salmon artfully arranged amid light and lovely shirred eggs. Then puff pastry and country sausage, freshly squeezed orange

TRADE SECRETS FROM A THREE-STAR CHEF

juice (available with or without champagne), assorted breads, and imported spreadable fruits. You finish with a wild cherry clafouti served with creme fraiche and espresso. Just before five-o'clock, everyone takes a quick dip in the pool before departure.

Another five miles east lies another country—East Hampton, home to Hollywood producers, investment bankers, with an occasional important scientist or heavy-hitting lawyer. There's nothing laid-back about East Hampton—prime court time at the local tennis clubs is 8 A.M. The homes here are the kinds of places, as the playwright Samuel Kaufmann once observed, God would have created if he'd had the money.

Everyone at East Hampton parties has a lean and hungry look, and one glance at the food explains why. Luncheon will probably be a nonalcoholic, low-fat, low-cal, high-fiber mélange of fruit and vegetable juices, bran muffins, and crudités.

And so, as the sun sinks slowly in the west, we see that the Hamptons are really a state of mind, or rather at least three states of mind. And from them we have chosen our own version of the ultimate Hamptons luncheon.

Chilled Herbed Gazpacho

A rule of thumb for serving light luncheon fare: Make it tasty. This marvelous gazpacho follows the rule with a complex blend of ingredients that create a surprising tanginess. And unlike other gazpachos—the simple tomato puree variety that bores you after three spoonfuls—this one has texture and a few surprises.

Two	6-ounce cans tomato puree
One	#10 can Sacramento tomato juice
2	cups tomato pulp, deseeded (taken from the tomatoes used in the stuffed tomato recipe, which follows)
2	cucumbers, cut in half, seeds removed, finely chopped
2	large green peppers, seeds and ribs removed, finely chopped
2	medium onions, finely chopped
2	medium zucchini, finely chopped
2	stalks celery, finely chopped
2	garlic cloves, minced
1	tablespoon cracked pepper
1	tablespoon salt
2	teaspoons hot sauce
2	tablespoons red wine vinegar
2	tablespoons celery seed
1	tablespoon fresh ground herbs of your choice (or 1/2 tablespoon dried)

Pour the tomato puree, tomato juice, and pulp into a Cuisinart or blender and process until smooth. Transfer to a large bowl, add the remaining ingredients, and stir until well blended. Taste and adjust the seasonings to your liking. Refrigerate for at least 3 hours.

Serve very cold. (See box for tips on presentation.)

VARIATION: You may substitute any crisp vegetables for those listed above—except for any member of the cabbage family, such as cabbage, Brussels sprouts, broccoli, cauliflower. They're too gassy for this recipe.

JELLY JARS AND FLOWERPOTS...

...make wonderful "bowls" for gazpacho. If you use jelly jars, add a small stalk of celery as garnish. Choose clear Lucite flowerpots, available at your local nursery, and top with cucumber rounds. Mason jars work well, too— garnish with a stalk of fennel or a scallion.

THE ULTIMATE HAMPTONS LUNCHEON

HOW TO CHOP AN ONION

Efficient chefs know there's only one correct way to chop an onion: Using a *very sharp* knife, slice the onion in half, lay the open side down, slice in horizontal layers, then lengthwise, then across.

Tomates Farcies à la Riz

In the Hamptons (as elsewhere), it's always a plus if you can serve something that's French or at least sounds foreign or exotic. That's why no one at The Station ever knew that this recipe for rice-stuffed tomatoes originated in Chippewa Falls, Wisconsin.

4–6	plump vine-ripened tomatoes, washed and patted dry
2	tablespoons extra-virgin olive oil
2	cloves garlic, minced
1	medium onion, finely chopped
1	cup uncooked rice, preferably Uncle Ben's long-grain
2	cups vegetable stock, your own or low-sodium canned
1/2	cup currants
2	tablespoons curry powder
1/4	teaspoon pepper
1/4	teaspoon salt
1	pinch saffron
	Parsley or cilantro sprigs for garnish

With a sharp knife, cut off the tops of the tomatoes so that you have an opening of 1 1/2 to 2 inches in diameter. Using a small spoon,* scoop out the pulp (save it for the gazpacho recipe). The tomato "shell" that remains should be about 1/4 inch thick.

Salt the interior of the tomatoes, turn them upside down, and place on paper toweling. Set aside for at least 20 minutes, until the excess liquid is drawn out.

In a 2 1/2-quart saucepan, pour the olive oil and sauté the garlic and onions in the olive oil until the onions are transparent. Add the rice and coat well with oil. Add the vegetable stock and

*A grapefruit spoon works well because of its serrated edges.

TRADE SECRETS FROM A THREE-STAR CHEF

bring to a boil. Add the currants, curry powder, pepper, salt, and saffron. Turn the heat to low, cover the pan, and simmer until all the liquid is absorbed—about 15 minutes. *Do not stir* while cooking.

After the rice is done and has cooled to room temperature, fluff it with a fork. A spoonful at a time, carefully stuff each tomato to the top, then add a bit more to create a gentle mound.

Garnish with parsley or cilantro and serve at room temperature.

TIP: If a tomato does not stand straight, slice off a bit from the bottom to level it.

Farcie

CURIOUS ABOUT CURRY?

Curry powders are a blend of many herbs and spices—among them tumeric, Moroccan coriander, cumin, ginger, nutmeg, fennel, cinnamon, fenugreek, white pepper, cardamom, cloves, Tellicherry black pepper, Spanish saffron, nutmeg, and caraway. *Sweet* curry powder is mild and not too spicy; *hot* is similar to sweet but has more hot red pepper and ginger; *garam masala* is considered all-purpose; and *maharajah* style contains Spanish saffron and is thought to be the best—it's also the most expensive (in 1992, maharajah-style curry sold for $5.95 for *1/28th of an ounce*).

NOTE: If you're new to curry, use it sparingly until you become accustomed to the exotic flavor. But do experiment with it in other dishes, particularly lamb, pork, poultry, and potatoes.

Madame Poullard's Omelette

This phenomenal omelette was the signature dish of a restaurant in Normandy known as La Mer Poullard, which was situated at the base of the great St. Michel. Madame Poullard, who created this omelette, died several years ago at a venerable age, but her legend lives on in this recipe.

YIELD: SERVES 6

10	*fresh eggs, at room temperature, separated*
4	*tablespoons sweet butter, melted and clarified*
	Salt and pepper
4	*tablespoons heavy cream, whipped*
1/8	*cup chopped parsley*

Beat the egg yolks with a whisk until well blended; beat the whites with an electric mixer until soft peaks start to form.

In a 10-inch sauté pan, heat the butter on medium high until it begins to sizzle. Pour in the yolks and season with salt and pepper. When the yolks begin to set, add the whipped cream and then the egg whites and blend quickly, using a spatula. Turn the heat to high and let the egg mixture cook for 3–4 minutes while you move the pan back and forth over the flame.

Using a spatula, gently lift the edge of the omelette to check the bottom. When speckled with brown, lower the heat to medium and use the spatula to fold the omelette in half. Allow it to cook for one more minute, then slide it onto a serving plate.

Serve immediately, sprinkled with chopped parsley.

VARIATIONS: For a broccoli and mushroom omelette, blanch the broccoli until tender, refresh it with cold water, and set it aside. Sauté the mushrooms in a little butter until cooked through.

Just before folding, spoon the broccoli and mushrooms onto one side of the omelette, then fold the other side over it. Serve immediately.

NOTE: *This recipe is versatile. Add diced chicken or ham before folding the omelette, or bits of bacon, or blanched green peppers, or whatever appeals to you.*

THE GREAT OMELETTE PAN DEBATE

It's a never-ending argument among cooks: Should you use your omelette pan *only* for omelettes and then never wash it? Or should you throw caution to the wind and simply use a multipurpose Teflon-coated pan, take care to avoid scratches, and clean up with soap and water?

We're dogmatic on this one: Reserve your special pan only for omelettes and—if you're serious about omelette making—learn how to flip them (see box). Reason: The moment you scratch the pan with a spatula, the pan is finished: liquid will nestle in the tiny scratches and the omelette will adhere to the pan so that you can't turn it. After each use, wipe out the pan with paper toweling before storing.

Rum Raisin–Walnut Ice Cream

Of course you can purchase an ice cream like this from Häagen Dazs or Ben & Jerry's if you're pressed for time, but why not knock everyone's socks off by making your own?

1/2	cup raisins
1/4	cup dark rum
1	cup sugar
8	egg yolks
2 1/2	cups milk
2 1/2	cups heavy cream
1/2	cup walnuts, coarsely chopped

Soak the raisins in the rum for at least 6 hours or overnight.

In a large bowl, beat together the sugar and egg yolks until they lighten in color. In a medium sauce pan, heat the milk to almost boiling, then slowly pour it into the bowl with the sugar and yolks, beating constantly. Allow the mixture to cool.

Add the whipping cream, raisins, and walnuts to the mixture. Refrigerate until cold. Then pour into an ice cream machine and follow the manufacturer's instructions. If you don't own a machine, see the box below.

Serve immediately.

NOTE: *Any rum that did not get absorbed by the raisins should be added* after *the ice cream has been processed to the desired consistency. If you add it before, the alcohol will interfere with the freezing, and you'll end up with ice cream* soup.

DO-AHEAD MISCELLANY

—The gazpacho can be made a day ahead. Keep it covered and refrigerated until ready to serve.

—You may prepare the ingredients for the stuffed tomatoes up to a day ahead, but don't stuff them until 2 hours before serving. Keep the tomatoes wrapped in plastic and the rice in a covered bowl.

—Ice cream may be made days ahead. Allow it to sit at room temperature for about 15 minutes so that it softens slightly before serving.

NOTE: *Except (obviously) for the ice cream, the items on this menu do not freeze well.*

4

Cooking for the Enemy

A MENU TO PLEASE THE FUSSIEST OF GUESTS

Sometimes, before you can understand the flavor of the food, you must understand the seasoning of the chef. Here is Anne at her most piquant:

"I love cooking at the height of rush hour when my powers of concentration are pushed to the limit. It's then that my kitchen really comes alive; I feel I'm in the midst of a glorious theatrical production, with me as the star! During those hectic moments of juggling a thousand details, the last thing I want to think about is the *dramatis personae* assembling beyond my swinging doors. But this is nearly impossible when you cook in a place like the Hamptons; our little towns are full of celebrities and food aficionados who want to insert themselves into my one-woman show.

"This year, I've decided to award a private Oscar for Most Difficult Customer. And the winner is...the frail but formidable Madame X, who handed the waiter a signed affidavit from her doctor stating that if Madame's palate should come in contact with any of a zillion ingredients such as peppers, tomatoes, garlic, butter, nuts of any kind, and on and on—not only would a near-death experience result, but also all manner of medical personnel, ambulance drivers, resuscitation experts, probably even coroners, would be upon us in moments. In short, it would be *my* fault if the lady expired while dining in my restaurant.

"Of course you would expect that I remained professional

Leek and Potato Soup

Salmon Fillets with Honey-Mustard Glaze

Fresh String Beans and Roasted Garlic with Sliced Baguettes

Fresh Strawberries with Balsamic Vinegar and Cracked Black Pepper

SERVES 4–6

and calm. That I stood by stoically and reassured my fussy customer that we could accommodate even the most neurotic of palates. Wrong: I went quietly berserk! Shouldn't this woman be fed in a hospital, I sneered. No, I hissed, that wouldn't be proper—didn't she really require the services of a mental institution? Well, thank God the waiter blocked the door to the kitchen, thus preventing me from personally speeding her demise right then and there.

"Once I regained my composure, I did what any seasoned stage actor does when playing to a hostile audience: I improvised. Quickly I glanced about the kitchen, searching for a solution. There they were: mustard, honey, sugar, and soy sauce— four ingredients that were *not* on Madame's list of forbidden foods. I whipped them together, used the mixture as a glaze on grilled salmon, and handed this new dish to the waiter to deliver. Within moments he returned with the verdict: 'Marvelous,' she'd said. 'And it doesn't taste as fishy as most fish.'

"Though I haven't seen Madame X for many months now, I think of her often—rather fondly, in fact. That's because my impromptu glazed salmon entrée became *the* most popular fish specialty on my restaurant menu."

The next time you find yourself having to cook for the enemy, give this recipe a try. The only drawback: Guests may want to come to your home more often!

FRESH CHIVES AT YOUR FINGERTIPS

Here's an easy and inexpensive way to keep chives at the ready. Buy two shallots and fill a small pot with fresh earth. Plant the shallots root end down, keep the soil damp and put them in a sunny window. Within a few weeks, your home-grown chives will be ready for snipping.

Leek and Potato Soup

This soup is considered by most people in the restaurant business to be the world's favorite. It is also the classic base for most French soups (see note), and an elegant starter for this particular menu.

3	large Idaho potatoes, peeled and cut into medium-size pieces
3	medium-size leeks,* washed very well; white part only, cut into rounds
1	quart water
1 1/2	cubes Knorr's Chicken Base†
	Freshly ground pepper
2	tablespoons fresh minced chives

Combine the potatoes, leeks, water, and chicken base cubes in a 2 1/2-quart pot. Bring to a boil, season with pepper, reduce the heat, and simmer until the potatoes and leeks are soft, about 25 minutes.

In a food processor or blender, puree the soup (in batches if necessary) and return it to the original pot. Taste and adjust the seasoning. Reheat very slowly. Serve with fresh minced chives sprinkled on top.

THE ULTIMATE SOUP BASE?

That's the leek and potato soup you'll prepare for this menu. It's the classic base of most French soups, and once you've mastered it, you can easily make any of the following:

—Vichyssoise (add heavy cream until the color is almost white, then chill)
—Watercress soup (add 2 small bunches cleaned and stemmed, and puree along with leeks and potatoes)
—Broccoli soup (add 2 cups cleaned florets and tenderest stems and puree with the other ingredients)
—Cream of broccoli soup (do as above, then add heavy cream until the soup lightens in color)

It's fun to experiment with new soups, too. With leek and potato as your base, you can add a variety of ingredients, such as asparagus, pureed as above. Use your imagination!

---

*You may use medium-size onions if you wish, but be aware that the taste will not be as subtle.

†One of the rare occasions when a cube (plus water) is preferable to canned or homemade stock. The cube provides the added oomph needed for this soup.

Salmon Fillets with Honey-Mustard Glaze

This recipe is the essence of simplicity. It takes just seconds to prepare, and once you master the trade secret of proper glaze application (you'll do it expertly on your first try), you'll create a gorgeous looking dish with that restaurant taste and appearance.

PREHEAT THE BROILER.

1	tablespoon Dijon mustard
1	tablespoon sugar
2	tablespoons honey
3	tablespoons Kikkoman soy sauce
4–6	salmon fillets
Optional:	1 bunch cilantro, washed and dried

Blend the condiments together thoroughly with a whisk and set aside. When the broiler is ready, arrange the *unsalted, unpeppered, unglazed* salmon fillets on the broiler pan and place beneath the flame. After about 4 1/2 minutes, carefully brush each fillet with the honey-mustard glaze. Return to the broiler and cook another 2 minutes, or until the salmon feels firm to the touch.

After placing the broiled salmon on serving plates (garnished with cilantro if you wish), gently brush the fish with the glaze one more time. This last-minute, final application is the key to a rich-looking, beautiful, shiny glaze. Serve immediately.

VARIATION: You're going to like this glaze so much, we recommend you double the recipe and keep it on hand for a variety of uses. Using the same two-step glazing application, it's excellent with chicken or pork, or on any firm-fleshed fish such as sword-

fish, monkfish, codfish, or haddock. (*The broiling time will be the same as long as pieces are approximately 1/2 inch thick.*)

Because of its sweetness, this glaze is not recommended for beef or veal. Nor is it recommended for tuna; the glaze darkens tuna so that it doesn't look very appetizing.

NOTE: *To avoid an unpleasant mixture of flavors, keep the glaze* pure—*i.e. don't apply the glaze that you used for salmon to chicken, or vice versa. Just pour the amount you need into a bowl and leave the rest in the jar, tightly covered.*

SALT SECRETS

In your arsenal of seasonings, salt may well be the most powerful, least understood, and most overused. In the culinary sense, it can bring food to life, but it also can be deadly: When used excessively, it will destroy any dish—and there's very little you can do to rectify the damage. That's why we urge home cooks to follow these tips about salt (and other seasonings): (1) Taste foods *often* while you're cooking and *always* taste before adding salt. (2) When in doubt, don't! You can always add more later, but you never can take it away!

One reason many cooks oversalt is because they simply do not understand *how to taste food.* If you're using only the tip of your tongue to sample a soup or sauce, you're reaching only a small fraction of your tastebuds. Savor food with the tip, the top, and the sides of the tongue as well. (It goes without saying that the serious home cook also will be evaluating a "work-in-progress" by using all the other senses, too!)

RULE OF THUMB: *Cook with as little salt as possible, and allow your guests to do their own judicious seasoning at the table. If a dish requires salt in its preparation, we encourage guests to "test it" first before automatically salting, which a surprising number of people still do today. One wonders: Perhaps the sight of a salt shaker triggers an involuntary reaction of the hand?*

Fresh String Beans and Roasted Garlic with Sliced Baguettes

Brace yourself: We're going to prepare string beans properly (not the way your mother used to make them).

NOTE: *When you serve them with oven-roasted garlic and a baguette—a combination your guests probably will not ever have had, or at least not lately—you will have created an unusual and memorable course. Amazingly, the roasting process mellows the taste of the garlic and eliminates its strong odor.*

For the beans:

1   teaspoon sugar

1   teaspoon salt

2   pounds fresh string beans or French haricots verts, rinsed well with stem ends removed. (Don't remove the long slender tendrils; they're rather pretty, and edible, so why take them off?)

1   tablespoon extra-virgin olive oil

   Salt and pepper to taste

Fill a 2-quart pot with water and bring to a boil. Add the sugar and salt and boil for 10 seconds, then add the string beans and cook 3–5 minutes. The beans should still be crisp! Remove from the heat, drain immediately, then rinse the beans quickly under cold water to stop the cooking process; drain again and set aside.

Just before serving, toss the beans in a sauté pan with the olive oil until heated through. Add salt and pepper to taste.

For the garlic:

PREHEAT THE OVEN TO 350°.

    4 to 6   *large heads garlic,* unpeeled, cut in half horizontally*
    4 to 6   *tablespoons extra-virgin olive oil*
            Salt and pepper

In a small baking pan, place the cut heads of garlic; dribble the oil over all and season with salt and pepper. Place in the oven and roast for 30 minutes. Remove from the oven and cool to room temperature. *Do not refrigerate.*

SERVING TIP: Serve the garlic as is, on a small serving plate with cocktail forks, one per person. Instruct your guests to pluck one or several cloves, squeeze the garlic from its natural wrapping, and spread it on a baguette slice.

A FEW WORDS ABOUT VEGETABLES

Never, never, never use the canned variety—they're inexcusable, inedible, and also the sign of an uncaring amateur. When you can get fresh, buy fresh. But when you can't, there are two—and only two—frozen vegetables that are acceptable (if, that is, you're serious about cooking). They are: Tiny or baby peas (plain, not adorned with onions or bathed in butter sauce) and corn, ungarnished. Frozen peas may even be preferable to fresh in certain recipes, because they are always uniform in size (not to mention so simple to get at). You'll see what we mean when you try the French recipe using frozen peas in Chapter 8.

NOTE: *This caveat does not always apply to the tomato, which is, after all, botanically a* berry *and therefore a type of fruit.*

---

*If your guests are garlic lovers, add another head or two (and just use more oil—about 1 tablespoon per head of garlic.) Don't be tempted to buy the huge variety known as "elephant" garlic—it has a woody texture and is virtually tasteless.

NOTES ABOUT TASTES AND TEXTURES

Earlier in the book, we emphasized the importance of including a balance of tastes and textures in every menu, and we've done it with this meal as well. Here's the logic: Soup is soft and so is salmon, so we want the beans to be crisp and the baguettes to be nice and chewy. The soup and salmon are mellow-tasting, so we've provided a contrast to the soup's slightly salty flavor by using a sweet glaze on the salmon. The sweet taste of green beans is an excellent foil for the pungent garlic. And of course, our dessert of strawberries with balsamic vinegar and pepper is an incredible four-senses experience that speaks, quite eloquently, for itself.

BREAD ETIQUETTE

You certainly may serve bread any way you wish, but if you want to stick to the European way of doing things, here are a few tips:

—Since the first course will usually be starchy, wait to serve your bread until the second course, as we did with the salmon and string beans.
—To serve, slice it in the kitchen and then bring it to the table on one plate; guests can serve themselves and may either rest their piece of bread on their plate, or put it on the tablecloth. (If you think it's romantic to "break bread" at the table, go ahead; but have your Dirt Devil ready to clean up the millions of crumbs that will be flying in every direction.)
—Most important: Do not serve butter with your bread. To do so is incorrect (according to Europeans, who serve butter with bread only at breakfast or, on occasion, with certain raw vegetables such as radishes). It's also overkill, we think, to serve butter with this menu in particular, where garlic (roasted with olive oil) is being spread liberally on the baguette. Moreover, most other menus have sauces or other liquids that can be sopped up with bread, so even the guest who can't fathom butterless bread will still be satisfied.

Fresh Strawberries with Balsamic Vinegar and Cracked Black Pepper

This recipe is a superb example of what happens when you combine everyday ingredients with something unexpected—such as black pepper. The result: A sophisticated taste sensation!

2	quarts ripe fresh strawberries, rinsed, hulled, and sliced vertically (to maintain the shape of the fruit)
3	tablespoons sugar
1/4	cup balsamic vinegar
	Cracked black pepper

Mix the sliced strawberries with the sugar and let stand for 30 minutes unrefrigerated.

Just before serving, toss the strawberries with the balsamic vinegar in a large bowl.

To serve, with slotted spoon, scoop the strawberries into 12-ounce red wineglass. Add a pinch of cracked black pepper on top of each serving.

WHEN IS UGLY BEAUTIFUL?

When you're judging strawberries. Remember, as with most things anatomical, big doesn't necessarily mean good. Often, the sweetest, most delicious berries are small and even misshapen. If in doubt about flavor, you may absolutely ask your greengrocer if you may taste one before you buy them. Why should you spend $3.99 or more for a quart of strawberries that are pulpy and taste like cotton batting?

NOTE: Contrary to what you may have heard, adding sugar to pulpy strawberries or macerating them in sugar for more than half an hour will only make matters worse: the sugar draws out precious liquids, which will eventually collect at the bottom of the bowl where they won't do your recipe any good.

GOOD TO THE LAST DROP

Coffee is a wonderful way to end almost any meal, but *when* you serve it can make or break the meal. With this menu, for example, serve coffee *after* the strawberries, so that the palate doesn't become a battleground for hot and cold or bitter and sweet. Indeed, the singular taste of the strawberries with balsamic vinegar will be destroyed by the taste of coffee, whether you take it black, with cream or sugar, or with both.

Speaking of varied combinations, encourage your guests to try taking their after-dinner coffees with only *one* addition—i.e., one or the other but not both. Haven't you noticed that many people treat coffee not as a food but as a milkshake? We say, if it tastes like it was made at a soda fountain, don't bring it to the dinner table!

DO-AHEAD MISCELLANY

—You can make the leek and potato soup the day before your party; just keep it covered in the refrigerator overnight, remove midafternoon the following day, and allow it to come to room temperature.

—Because the honey-mustard glaze is a snap to make, consider preparing a large batch ahead of time to have on hand. Keep it in a tightly covered jar, unrefrigerated.

—The fresh string beans can be blanched ahead of time and kept at room temperature. (Don't forget to refresh them in cold water to stop the cooking process or you'll wind up with limp beans.)

—You may roast the garlic up to one hour ahead of time, but place it in a warm oven for 10 minutes before serving.

—Start the strawberries macerating about a half hour before you're planning to serve them.

NOTE: *The items on this menu do not freeze well.*

TRADE SECRETS FROM A THREE-STAR CHEF

5

Presentation Is Everything

BUT FOOD IS *NOT* A TOY!

*I*f you've ever been to one of those huge buffets that hotels sometimes call "luaus," you've probably marveled at the amount of food available and wondered who was responsible for presenting it in such bad taste: endless rings of pineapple slices encircling maraschino cherries; giant mounds of liver pâté shaped to resemble a sitting hen; platters of tired sliced meats layered on exhausted lettuce; and the inevitable swan ice sculpture, water dripping from its beak onto the steam table of soggy vegetables.

Now, alas, the trendiest American restaurants are doing even more violence to the concept of presentation. To wit, a description of one such table d'hôte:

"Subtly flavored, coarsely chopped tuna is unmolded in a perfect disk and encircled with a light tomato emulsion. Decoratively set atop the tuna are perfectly trimmed 'petals' of softened yellow and green bell peppers, alternated with 'petals' of the rosy red tuna. The house's own smoked salmon is lightly pressed to cover exactly the surface of a square plate like a layer of enamel. On top of the salmon is a little lump of cucumber salad with salmon roe and a bit of caviar."

What about dessert? "Chocolate mousse comes in the form of a tall soldier's hat with straps of marzipan and a brim of

---

Lightly Curried Fresh Pea Soup

Rack of Lamb

Sauté of Julienned Vegetables

Lemon Mousse with Raspberry Sauce

SERVES 4–6

chocolate. A tiny white peach Bavarian is dwarfed by a decorative chocolate superstructure patterned after a Japanese well."

You can't make this stuff up. These are actual unedited descriptions of, um, food served at a real restaurant on the East Coast that was reviewed by Andy Birsh in the February 1993 issue of *Gourmet* magazine. And by the way, first courses range from $12 to $25, main courses are $28 to $39, a seven-course tasting dinner is fixed at $110 per person, and desserts are $10 to $13. According to the review, the place is wildly successful.

In our opinion, all this extravagance violates every principle of traditional presentation, which is based on subtle visual enhancement of the qualities inherent in the meal to be served. Food is not a toy. A buffet is not a Lego-block construction. Food is—or should be—a sensory delight. How to do it? Look for ways to augment, to flatter, the virtues of the meal. Let's consider the menu at hand:

The first course, pea soup, is a lovely green, but it's rather plain all by itself. It needs an embellishment—a special garnish that will provide a contrasting color and an interesting flavor and texture. One might consider a few croutons, preferably homemade; a sprinkling of cayenne or paprika; a sprig of any fresh herb; chopped bacon, or small, thin strips of bacon; strips of pimiento or pimiento "crossed" with a fresh herb; chopped celery or another firm vegetable (pepper or zucchini comes to mind); thin half-slices of cucumber or lemon; chopped egg; grated cheese; slivered almonds; a dollop of sour cream or creme fraiche. The list can go as far as your imagination.

Rack of lamb is rather easy—there are all those lovely ribs to work with, but don't succumb to the temptation to use those silly little booties. Instead, if you're serving two racks on a platter, stand them up and interlock the ribs for a dramatic effect. Or you can cut one rack in half and serve it the same way. If you prefer serving on individual plates, slice the rack into chops and lay one down on the plate, then top it with another chop positioned at an angle. If you want to add texture and color, try a sprinkling of sautéed bread crumbs and chopped parsley. Or surround the rack with the sautéed julienned vegetables—the greens and oranges and yellows will provide a striking contrast.

Lemon mousse with raspberry sauce—it makes you want to enroll in a class entitled Sauce Painting 101. It's easy to "paint" with a sauce—and the effect can be quite dramatic. A few ideas: Pour 1/4 cup of sauce onto a plate and rotate the plate until you've created a circle of sauce about 4–5 inches in diameter. Scoop the mousse into the center, then drizzle additional sauce down the sides of the mousse. Or start with a circle of sauce, then place a teaspoonful of mousse (beaten first so it's slightly melted) in the center of the circle. Place the tip of a knife in the center of the mousse and pull it through the raspberry sauce toward the edges of the mousse. You might also try scooping the mousse into a balloon-type wineglass or another lovely vessel, and drizzle the sauce over it. Or experiment with a parfait-type presentation, with alternating layers of sauce and mousse.

The presentation of food can be an art form, one that showcases your culinary talents and creativity. Perhaps more than that, it's a form of communication: even the smallest, subtlest touches can show guests that you have made an effort—that you took the time to care.

PRESENTATION AND THE PURLOINED PHEASANT

Of course, presentation is part and parcel of ambience, the whole panorama of sights and sounds and smells one savors in a truly fine restaurant. Not only how the food is served but how the maître d' treats us, how the waitstaff attends to our needs, is what carries us away. However, one must take care not to get *too* carried away. Harken to this cautionary tale of a visit Anne once made to Laserre, one of her favorite French restaurants: "This was about a thousand years ago, so some of the details are a bit fuzzy. In fact I can't even recall who picked up the whopper of a bill that evening; was it my husband or his business associate? It doesn't matter—I do remember that this was one of the most beautiful places I'd ever been. It was a profusion of pink linens and splendid wild flowers and Baccarat crystal and gold Vermeille flatware. And then there was that incredible ceiling—it opened silently every twenty minutes or so to allow the smokers' exhalations to float gently up and out of the room. For a moment or two, you were under the stars and thought you'd died and gone to heaven. (Of course when it rained, the ceiling remained shut and you had to suffer with the deadly smoke, but a serving of white asparagus usually made up for it.)

"On every table, a small elegant pewter pheasant was placed. With its long curving tail and hand-etched detail, it really was the perfect centerpiece—so unusual, so striking, so unlike anything I'd seen in shops at home in Great Neck, New York. In fact, so taken was I with this little bird, I decided to steal it. Having had a lot of practice pilfering ashtrays as a teenager, I knew precisely how to purloin the pheasant: I carefully looked around in my most sophisticated fashion and slipped it into my handbag.

"Out of nowhere, almost immediately, the maître d' appeared at our table. 'Bon soir, madame,' he said with a smile. Then he proceeded to entertain me with a fairy tale—told entirely in French, of course—about a little pheasant who was forced to leave his nest, and not only that, his family and his friends and his country too. It was so very, very sad, he said, that the very thought of it brought him to tears.

"Before he was forced to *show* me the tears—and by this time I was thanking the baby Jesus that no one else at the table understood French—I thanked him for sharing such a touching story and slipped the pheasant back onto the table.

"Of course, I was mortified by the experience, but the man handled the situation so perfectly, with such class, that in a way it was the perfect ending to the evening. Mind you, I'd never try that stunt again; I understand that nowadays when a pheasant is missing from your table at Laserre, they automatically add a hundred-dollar charge to your bill."

Lightly Curried Fresh Pea Soup

This is a soup you can make all year round. (Because it's not a traditional pea soup made from dried peas, we use the term "fresh"—which, of course, they were before they were frozen.)

One	*24-ounce bag of frozen baby peas*
1	*quart chicken stock (preferably your own)*
1	*medium onion, coarsely chopped*
1	*tablespoon curry powder, preferably garam masala, added in increments or to taste*

In a 2 1/2-quart pot, place the peas and half the stock. Bring to a boil, lower the heat, and add the chopped onion. Cook until the onion and peas are soft, about 5–7 minutes. Remove from the heat and let the mixture cool for at least 20 minutes.

Transfer the mixture to a blender and, with the motor on, add the rest of the stock, a half-cup at a time, until the soup coats a wooden spoon. (As soon as the soup coats the spoon, stop adding stock.) Continue to blend and add the curry, a half-teaspoon at a time. Taste and then add another half-teaspoon, taste again, and repeat until the flavor suits you.

Pour the mixture back into the pot and heat until hot. Serve immediately.

NOTE: *For more information about curry, see page 33.*

If you've got a great butcher, just tell him you want your rack(s) of lamb prepared so that they're "ready for broiling"—he'll know what to do. Otherwise, specify that you want him to (1) remove the outer layer of fat; (2) break the large "back" bone (so you needn't bring a hatchet to the table); (3) do a French treatment of the bones (which means he'll shave off the fat and gristle so they'll look pretty).

How much lamb to buy? Most racks of lamb will have 7 or 8 ribs, which means you'll have seven or eight chops. Depending on the quantity of meat on a chop—not to mention your guests' appetites—you may want to purchase an additional rack or two.

Rack of Lamb

You may not serve rack of lamb often because of the expense, but when you do, your guests will be eternally grateful.

PREHEAT THE OVEN TO 425°.

1   rack of lamb for four people or 2 racks for six, prepared by your butcher (see box, Lamb Talk)

1   clove garlic per rack, crushed

1   tablespoon extra-virgin olive oil per rack

1   tablespoon rosemary per rack

1   tablespoon cracked pepper per rack

Rub the rack(s) with garlic, then brush lightly with olive oil. Sprinkle with rosemary, then pepper. Cover the rib ends with foil.

Place the rack(s) fatty side up in a large pan and roast in the preheated oven for 15 minutes. Then turn over and roast another 10 minutes. Remove from the oven and set aside.

When ready to serve, turn the oven to broil. Place the rack(s) 4–5 inches from the heat source, meaty side up, until browned—about 3–5 minutes. *Do not overcook: lamb should be pink.* Serve immediately with Dijon mustard.

NOTE: *Do not—repeat—do not serve mint jelly with this or any other lamb dish!*

Sauté of Julienned Vegetables

Here's a classic example of a vegetable dish that's not only tasty, but beautiful too.

Wash the following vegetables, deseed where necessary, and then julienne either by hand or in your Cuisinart:

2   *medium-size carrots, peeled*

2   *medium-size zucchini*

2   *medium-size yellow squash*

1   *large red pepper, seeds and ribs removed*

1   *large green pepper, seeds and ribs removed*

3   *tablespoons extra-virgin olive oil*

1   *tablespoon sweet butter*

1   *clove garlic, minced*

1   *teaspoon sugar*

Salt and pepper to taste

Blanch the julienned carrots until crisp-tender and set aside with the rest of the uncooked vegetables.

In a large sauté pan, heat the olive oil and butter on a medium-high flame until bubbling, then add the garlic and sugar and stir-fry for about 30 seconds. Add the julienned vegetables and stir-fry for 3–4 minutes, stirring constantly. Season with salt and pepper and serve immediately.

What's lemon zest? It's
what you get when you scrape
or peel the outer (yellow) skin
of a lemon. Because the zest
contains oil, its flavor is more
intense than the juice. The
layer beneath the zest is called
the pith—it's white and bitter
and shouldn't be used.
(Lemon zesters are available
at most kitchenware stores.)

Lemon Mousse with Raspberry Sauce

*The trick to making a light and fluffy lemon mousse is using
very cold heavy cream. See box for a cautionary tale.*

For the mousse:

1	*package Knox unflavored gelatin*
5	*jumbo eggs, separated*
3/4	*cup sugar plus 1 1/2 tablespoons, preferably "instant dissolving sugar"*
1/2	*cup fresh lemon juice*
2	*tablespoons fresh lemon zest (see "Lemon Aid")*
1	*tablespoon Grand Marnier*
1/8	*teaspoon cream of tartar*
	Pinch of salt
1	*cup cold heavy cream*

Place the gelatin, egg yolks, and 3/4 cup of sugar into a mixing bowl and beat with an electric mixer until light and fluffy. Pour this mixture into a saucepan, add the lemon juice and zest, and heat on low, mixing constantly, until the sugar is completely dissolved. Remove from the heat and allow to cool, then blend in the Grand Marnier.

Using an electric mixer or whisk, beat the egg whites until foamy, then add the cream of tartar and pinch of salt and beat again until soft peaks form. Set aside.

Pour the *cold* whipping cream into a bowl, add the remaining 1 1/2 tablespoons sugar, and whip. Gently fold the lemon mixture into the whipped cream, then fold in the beaten egg whites.

Pour the mousse into a large bowl or an 8-cup decorative

mold and refrigerate for at least 4 hours. See chapter introduction for serving suggestions.

For the raspberry sauce:

10	*ounces frozen raspberries*
1/2	*cup sugar*

Place the frozen raspberries in a medium saucepan on medium heat. Melt completely, then add the sugar and continue to cook on medium until the sugar is dissolved.

Remove from the heat and allow to come to room temperature. Using a chinois or a fine sieve, strain out the raspberry seeds.

Use the sauce to "paint" the mousse as discussed in the introduction of this chapter.

DO-AHEAD MISCELLANY

—If you prepare the soup the morning of your party, reduce the curry by half (since it will grow stronger throughout the day). Do not refrigerate. Just before serving, taste, and add more curry if necessary.

—You may season and oil the lamb several hours ahead of time. Up to 2 hours ahead, you may precook the rack(s) as described in recipe. Cover loosely and keep at room temperature until ready to finish under the broiler.

—You may julienne the vegetables several hours before serving. Keep tightly wrapped in the refrigerator, then bring to room temperature just before stir-frying.

—You may prepare the lemon mousse in the morning. Keep it tightly covered and in the refrigerator until ready to serve.

NOTE: *The raspberry sauce freezes well, but the rest of the items in this menu do not.*

6

Nostalgia Without the Heartburn

A JEWISH DINNER FOR FRIDAY AND A GENTILE SUPPER FOR SUNDAY

Oven-Braised
Brisket of Beef

Good-for-You
Potato Skins

Steamed Fresh
Broccoli

Fresh Lemon
Bars

SERVES 4–6

What's the difference between a brisket of beef and a pot roast? What separates a wonton from a ravioli? When is a kreplach really a dumpling? There is a commonality of food among all peoples; every culture has dishes that are basically the same, though they may differ in name or because of certain added ingredients. Case in point: Our Jewish dinner, which features brisket of beef, and our Gentile supper, which highlights old-fashioned pot roast. It's a menu we devised after taking a couple of trips down memory lane.

Anne: Although we weren't an observant religious family, our usual Friday night dinner was a kosher meal—well, maybe it's more truthful to say we didn't sit down to a hamburger and a glass of milk. Typically, the meal would begin with gefilte fish and/or matzoball soup, and then we'd be given a choice of chicken or beef brisket, either of which would have been cooked for at least three weeks. Then we'd have noodle pudding or potato pancakes. The meal would end with some kind of sweet dessert such as macaroons or apple cake, maybe some fruit, or a candy-like marzipan, and a glass of plum brandy for those who were still awake.

Nancy: On a Sunday night in the Bible Belt, we might start our meal with canned fruit cocktail and from there go to an ice-cold, iceberg lettuce salad covered with Russian or "blue" cheese dressing. Dad's pot roast was a specialty, cooked for 3 days (or so it seemed) in a large pressure cooker, which he kept on an old wooden table in a corner of our screened-in porch. Of course, all along he'd been adding vegetables to the broth—usually an assortment of cauliflower and carrots and potatoes; by the time they were served, they'd become almost indistinguishable from one another. Dessert was usually a guest's responsibility, which he or she took rather seriously: at the end of the evening, a white cardboard box would be brought into the room and opened with a great flourish to reveal either a gooey "mile-high" lemon meringue pie, or a storebought cake comprised of condensed milk, eggs, and not-quite-cooked dough, which was covered with at least five inches of lard-based frosting. We loved it—indigestion and all.

It was fun talking about those meals from the past. But we faced a challenge: how to put together a nostalgic meal that wouldn't be panned by health-conscious food critics or, more important, banned by the American Heart Association? We haven't done anything to change the brisket, which was extremely popular at The Station. But we've surrounded it with a collection of complementary family-style dishes that we think represent a perfect melding of memorable foods that won't kill you.

NOTE: *If you want to serve this meal European-style, start with the potato skins and serve the broccoli as a separate third course.*

Oven-Braised Brisket of Beef

This is one of the easiest recipes in the world; it's done entirely in the oven and tastes best if you prepare it in advance, preferably the morning of the day you plan to serve it.

A whole brisket is an enormous slab of meat, so make sure to ask your butcher for the "first cut"—it's the leanest part—then figure on a quarter pound per person, or more if you want leftovers for sandwiches or hash.

PREHEAT THE OVEN TO 325°.

1	package Lipton Onion Soup mix
1	first-cut beef brisket, 1/4 pound (or more) per person
2	cups Sacramento tomato juice
1	bottle high-quality beer
1	tablespoon cornstarch

Prepare your roasting pan (see Brisket Tips). Sprinkle the soup mix over the brisket and rub it into the meat. Place the brisket in the pan. Mix the tomato juice with the beer, then pour the mixture over brisket. Seal the roasting pan, place it in the oven, and roast for a minimum of 3 hours. (Figure on 40–50 minutes per pound of brisket.)

After removing from the oven, keep the brisket sealed and allow it to stand for 15 minutes before serving. Skim off any excess grease with a wooden spoon.

Just before serving, place the brisket on a cutting board and slice it against the grain 1/4 inch thick. Meanwhile, reheat the gravy slowly over a low flame (see box) and whisk in the cornstarch to thicken.

On a large platter, arrange the slices of brisket, then nap them with gravy. If you wish, decorate the border of the platter with the potato skins cut into quarters and garnished with parsley.

WHAT? A SOUP MIX FOR BRISKET?

We've said elsewhere in this book that homemade is *not* always best. Allow us to repeat ourselves with respect to the brisket recipe: to achieve the right flavor, you really must use Lipton's Onion Soup mix (no, we don't get a kickback). The dehydrated onions are the secret ingredient. There is *no* substitute—especially not fresh onions!

NEVER-FAIL SAUCE-THICKENING TIPS

Always use cornstarch, never flour, to thicken a tomato-based gravy. Flour will lump, whereas cornstarch produces a fine, smooth texture. The best way to thicken a large batch? Remove a cupful of *warm* gravy from the roaster, whisk in 1 tablespoon cornstarch, then return the gravy to the roaster and stir. Heat slowly for 3–5 minutes, until the gravy thickens.

BRISKET TIPS

—Brisket can dry out while it's roasting if it's not properly sealed. Years ago, we used to create a seal using a flour and water mixture that was a lot like paste; today there are easier ways to do it. First, use a heavy roasting pan and lid (a Le Creuset–type covered casserole is perfect), then place a double thickness of parchment or foil beneath the lid; this will keep moisture from escaping.

ALTERNATIVE: If you are not sensitive to what we call "the tinny taste of foil," you can completely line your roasting pan with heavy-duty aluminum foil, add all ingredients, then wrap the foil tightly around the prepared brisket and place the lid on the pot.

—Have you ever taken a juicy roast from the oven and sliced it immediately—only to discover that within minutes, the meat has become dry and tough? All cooked meats need time to rest—at least 15 minutes, depending on size—so that the juices have time to become evenly distributed and to "set." If you prepare the brisket early in the day, keep it covered so it doesn't lose precious moisture.

TRADE SECRETS FROM A THREE-STAR CHEF

Good-for-You Potato Skins

We're certain that, in the future, potato skins will become a nostalgia food from the nineties. They're good for you, too. This recipe calls for a scant amount of olive oil—and you'll add just a sprinkling of herbs so the taste of the potato is what you remember.

4–6	*large Idaho potatoes, scrubbed clean and pricked with a fork*
4–6	*tablespoons extra-virgin olive oil*
2–3	*teaspoons* herbes de Provence *(see box, right) or* fines herbes *(see page 184)*
	Salt and pepper to taste
Optional:	*parsley for garnish*

If using a conventional oven, bake the potatoes at 375° for one hour, or until tender. If using a microwave, nuke the potatoes according to the manufacturer's instructions. Set aside until cool enough to handle.

Cut each potato in half and scoop out the insides, leaving about 1/4 inch of potato. With a pastry brush, brush the insides of each potato half with olive oil, then sprinkle with herbs and salt and pepper.

Place in a 400° oven for 10–15 minutes, until the skins are hot and crisp. Serve immediately, garnished with parsley if you wish.

Elsewhere in this book, we've advised against microwaving potatoes instead of baking them because the skins become soggy (and frankly, we like our food molecules just the way nature intended them—unzapped). Exception: When making potato skins, because the final reheating crisps the skin.

MAKE YOUR OWN HERB MIXTURES

Last time we checked, a one-ounce jar of *herbes de Provence* cost $8. Why let them rob you? We say fight back and make your own, using equal amounts of dried (and crushed) bay leaves, cloves, lavender, rosemary, summer savory, and thyme. To create *fines herbes,* mix dried chervil, chives, parsley, and tarragon in equal amounts.

Steamed Fresh Broccoli

This is the most economical way to prepare broccoli because you use virtually all of it—florets, stems, even the stalk. Once you've tried it this way, you'll never throw out the stalk again.

1   head broccoli, washed and patted dry
     Water for steaming

Pull off and discard all leaves. With a sharp knife, slice off 1/2 inch from the bottom of the stalk. Cut off the florets at the point where the stems meet the stalk. Then peel and discard about 1/4 inch of the outer stalk. Slice the remaining stalk into rounds, or julienne it.

So that all the broccoli can be steamed evenly, layer the broccoli pieces in your steamer as follows: stalks on the bottom, stems next, florets on top. Steam for 5–7 minutes, until just barely tender.

Serve immediately. See box for serving and garnish ideas.

VEGETABLE TRICKS

—When steaming or blanching vegetables, remove them from the pot as soon as they are done—*never* leave the cover on the pot or the vegetables will continue to cook.

—When cooking vegetables that will be combined with other ingredients and reheated (the carrots for a pot pie, for example, or broccoli for a pasta dish), "refresh" them with cold water immediately when hot but still crisp. *Important:* Continue to refresh until the vegetables are cool to the touch, which may take more than a minute. A quick splash will *not* stop the cooking process

—For the brightest color, refresh green vegetables in an *ice water* bath.

NOSTALGIA WITHOUT THE HEARTBURN

Fresh Lemon Bars

These old-fashioned bars are a light and refreshing way to end a meal.

PREHEAT THE OVEN TO 350°.

For the crust:

1	cup all-purpose flour
1/4	cup confectioner's sugar
6	tablespoons sweet butter, melted

For the topping:

1	cup sugar
2	tablespoons flour
1/2	teaspoon baking powder
2	eggs, beaten (see box)
3	generous tablespoons fresh lemon juice
1	tablespoon lemon zest
	Confectioner's sugar for dusting
Optional:	Slivered lemon peel for garnish

Mix the flour, sugar, and butter together until well blended. Press the dough into an 8-inch square baking pan. Bake in the preheated oven for 20 minutes. Remove from the oven and cool. Do not turn off the oven.

Meanwhile, prepare the topping: Combine the sugar, flour, and baking powder. Add the beaten eggs and mix well. Add the lemon juice and zest and mix again. Pour over the cooled crust. Return the pan to the preheated oven for 25 minutes. Remove and cool slightly; slice while still warm. Dust with confectioner's sugar, and if you wish, decorate with slivers of lemon peel.

DO-AHEAD MISCELLANY

—For enhanced flavor, we encourage you to prepare your brisket in the morning. Keep it covered but *not* refrigerated. Reheat for about 10 minutes before serving.

—Bake (or microwave) the potatoes up to 2 hours ahead but do not halve or scoop out the flesh until shortly before crisping. Allow them to cool thoroughly, then cover with a tea towel or paper towels until ready to continue with recipe. Do not refrigerate.

—Broccoli can be cut early in the day; rinse with cold water, then place in plastic bags and refrigerate until a half-hour before steaming. You may also blanch the broccoli early in the day—for about 3–4 minutes, until heated but still crisp—and then steam (or blanch again) for 3–4 minutes just prior to serving.

—Make the Fresh Lemon Bars early in the day. Layer the bars on waxed paper and keep them in an air-tight tin until ready to serve.

NOTE: *The items on this menu do not freeze well.*

7

The Most Popular Restaurant Entrée of All Time

NO KIDDING, IT'S LIVER

*Y*up, liver. It's a favorite on the East End of Long Island—and in a moment, we're going to tell you why. But first, let us admit we know all too well that when one brings up the subject of "organ meat" with most Americans in the health-conscious nineties, one had better be braced for a barrage of negatives: "Worst possible thing for you unless you're anemic," friends will say as they shake their heads in disgust. "Killer cholesterol," others will note as they jab a finger at your chest. Occasionally, you'll even hear reasonably intelligent people babble that "it's just not right to eat this stuff." They think it's ghoulish—and, well, awful—to eat offal.

This is a tough crowd to reason with, but perhaps you can win them over by quoting M. F. K. Fisher, who may have been the most articulate at pleading the case for liver: "Why is it worse, in the end," she wrote, "to see an animal's head cooked and prepared for our pleasure than a thigh or a tail or a rib? If we are going to live on other inhabitants of this world we must not bind ourselves with illogical prejudices, but savor to the fullest the beasts we have killed.

"People who feel that a lamb's cheek is gross and vulgar

Salmon and Chive Cakes

Calve's Liver and Balsamic Onions

Garlicky Green Beans with Bread Crumbs

Chocolate Banana Tart

SERVES 4–6

when a chop is not are like the medieval philosophers who argued about such hairsplitting problems as how many angels could dance on the point of a pin. If you have these prejudices, ask yourself if they are not built on what you may have been taught when you were young and unthinking, and then if you can, teach yourself to enjoy some of the parts of an animal that are not commonly prepared."*

How to teach yourself to like calve's liver? Start by erasing all childhood memories of that horrid smell which comes from *beef* liver—it's the wrong kind of liver, being bigger, older, and tougher than that of a *calf*. Then forget about a certain shoe-leathery texture—it's caused by overcooking due to the erroneous belief that liver should be served well done. Of course, even if you can blot out these thoughts, you'll probably never be able to enjoy calve's liver at home—there will always be an unenlightened dissenter in the group, which is why so many people we know flock to restaurants to get their "fix."

And how delicious is it? You'll never know until you try Anne's famous version—the next time you're home alone.

First, prepare your palate with melt-in-your-mouth salmon and chive cakes.

*M. F. K. Fisher, *The Art of Eating.* Collier Books, New York, 1990, p. 271.

Salmon and Chive Cakes

These cakes are excellent as an appetizer, but when made into larger patties, they're also great for lunch or supper.

One	15-ounce can Alaska salmon
1	egg
1/2	cup finely chopped fresh chives
1/4	cup mayonnaise
1	tablespoon Dijon mustard
1	tablespoon capers, diced
1/4	cup minced shallots
1	teaspoon cracked black pepper
	A few drops of Louisiana Hot Sauce or Tabasco
1	cup unseasoned bread crumbs
1/2	cup vegetable oil, for cooking the cakes
2–3	lemons, each sliced into four wedges
Optional:	alfalfa sprouts for garnish

Carefully pick through the salmon and remove all bones. In a large ceramic bowl, mix the salmon with the egg, chives, mayonnaise, mustard, capers, shallots, pepper, hot sauce, and 1/2 cup of the bread crumbs.

With your hands, form the mixture into small patties—use a scant 1/4 cup for each patty. Then coat each side with the remaining bread crumbs and set aside.

In a large sauté pan, heat 1/4 cup of the oil on a medium flame until sizzling. Carefully place half the patties in the pan and cook each side about a minute and a half, or until golden brown. Remove from the pan and drain on paper toweling. Add the remaining oil to the pan and continue to sauté the remaining patties.

Serve immediately with 2 lemon wedges per person.

THE BEST CAPERS?

They're called nonesuch, and they come from the south of France. Yet another reason to live there.

VARIATION: For hot and spicy salmon cakes, add 1/2 teaspoon of chili-garlic paste to the mixture.

Calve's Liver and Balsamic Onions

*A*lthough calve's liver is quite delicious, it is not a great beauty. Therefore, serve it on a lovely white plate, and try some of the garnishing suggestions on page 73.

4 to 6	medium onions, sliced very thin
4 to 6	tablespoons sweet butter, plus 2 more tablespoons for sautéing onions
Two	1/4-inch slices of calve's liver per person, sinews removed (ask your butcher to prepare it this way)
1 to 1 1/2	cups flour
1 to 1 1/2	cups balsamic vinegar (about 1/4 cup for each serving)
	Sprigs of parsley, for garnish

Sauté the sliced onions in 2 tablespoons of butter until transparent and set aside.

In your largest sauté pan, place 1 tablespoon of butter for every 2 slices of liver that you can comfortably fit in the pan (the edges of the liver should not touch). Then heat on medium-high until the butter sizzles.

Quickly dredge both sides of each slice of liver in flour and shake off excess. Then sauté for 2 minutes on each side. Remove from the pan and place 2 slices of liver on each plate. Repeat the dredging and sautéing until all the liver is cooked.

In same sauté pan, with the heat on high, add the cooked onions and balsamic vinegar and toss for a few seconds until very hot. Then scoop up about 1/4 cup of this mixture for every 2 slices of liver and nap across the slices.

Garnish with lots of chopped parsley (or see box) and serve immediately.

NEW IDEAS FOR GARNISHES

If you want to really make a presentation statement—with calve's liver or other dishes that fall into the "ugly duckling" category—try these unusual and striking garnishes:

Peppery Confetti (also known as a *brunoise* of peppers): After deseeding, coring, and removing the white pith from 1 red, 1 green, and 1 yellow pepper, mince them as small as you can manage. Rinse with cold water, put in a towel, fold, and squeeze dry. Sprinkle this "confetti" across the platter or individual plates, then place your entree on top. Depending on what you're serving, you may find it interesting to sprinkle the confetti across, or on top of, your entrée.

NOTE: *Mincing a pepper is easier if you (1) cut it into long strips; (2) slice off, horizontally, any curved areas; (3) flatten the slices and stack them in small piles. Cut through, vertically, with a very sharp knife.*

Circle of Garnish: Instead of plunking a bit of herb on top of the entrée, use sections of herb—or baby greens—to decorate the *rim* of the plate. Or try edging the plate with deep fried zucchini, yellow squash, and leeks: With a "turning knife," cut the zucchini and squash into interesting shapes—stars, diamonds, triangles—and the leeks into rounds; then deep-fry until golden brown and drain on paper toweling.

Garlicky Green Beans with Bread Crumbs

By adding minced garlic for flavor and just enough bread crumbs for texture, you can transform ordinary green beans into a special dish.

1	pound green beans, washed, dried, stems removed
2	tablespoons extra-virgin olive oil
2	tablespoons sweet butter
1/2	tablespoon minced garlic
2	tablespoons unseasoned breadcrumbs

Have ready enough ice water to submerge the beans after cooking. Blanch the beans in boiling water for 2 to 3 minutes, until crisp-tender. Remove them from the stove and drain into a colander; plunge the colander into ice water to refresh the beans, then drain and set aside.

On a medium flame, heat the oil until bubbly, then add the butter and heat until melted. Add the minced garlic and sauté for 20 seconds. Add the bread crumbs and toss lightly in the oil, then add beans and toss until heated through.

Serve immediately.

TRADE SECRETS FROM A THREE-STAR CHEF

Chocolate Banana Tart

The combination of chocolate and bananas in this recipe is a winning one. Always follow the Chocolate Rule: the better the chocolate, the better the result. Use the highest quality available, such as Lindt Excellence, Valrhona, Callebaut, Guittard, or Ghirardelli.

PREHEAT THE OVEN TO 425°.

For the pastry:

1	cup flour
3/4	tablespoon sugar
1/4	teaspoon salt
1/4	cup plus 2 tablespoons chilled vegetable shortening or sweet butter
1	egg yolk
	Cold water

Please read about handling pie dough on page 198.

Sift the flour into a large bowl. Add the sugar and salt. With a pastry blender, work the shortening into the flour until the mixture resembles small peas. Add the egg yolk and mix with a fork. Sprinkle a little cold water onto the dough, then mix with your hands. If necessary, sprinkle more water and mix until you can gather the dough into a ball.

Place the dough on a work surface (preferably chilled marble) and gently knead it three times. Wrap it in plastic wrap and refrigerate for at least half an hour.

Remove the dough from the refrigerator and roll it out into a disk that is 1 inch larger than your pie pan. Gently pat it into the pan.

To prevent the dough from shrinking while in the oven, line

(Continued)

TWO TOOLS FOR CHOCOLATE

Grating chocolate by hand is a tedious, time-consuming job. Instead, use your Cuisinart, with metal blade attached. Break up large blocks of chocolate into 1/2-inch pieces, put in the work bowl, then pulse twice, stop and check, repeat pulsing, until chocolate looks finely grated.

TIP: *If you have trouble breaking up pieces of chocolate, an ice pick can help: just insert and pound down quickly but firmly.*

the shell with foil, then fill it with dry beans or marbles or clean pebbles.

Bake the pie shell in the preheated oven for 15 minutes. Scoop out the beans or pebbles and carefully remove the foil. Place the pie shell back in the oven for another 8–10 minutes so that the bottom is lightly browned. Remove and allow to cool.

PREHEAT THE OVEN TO 375°.

For the filling:

3	ripe but firm bananas, peeled and sliced into 1/4-inch rounds
3	ounces semisweet chocolate, finely grated (see box)
2	eggs
2	egg yolks
1/3	cup superfine sugar plus 2 tablespoons for topping
1/8	teaspoon salt
2	cups milk, scalded
1 1/2	teaspoons vanilla

Arrange banana slices on the prebaked crust. Sprinkle with the chocolate and set aside.

Place the eggs and yolks, 1/3 cup of the sugar, and the salt in a medium saucepan over a medium-low flame. With an electric mixer, beat until the consistency reaches the "ribbon" stage (see box). Turn the flame to medium-high and begin to whisk in the scalded milk, about a quarter cup at a time, until all has been incorporated and the mixture nearly comes to a boil. When the mixture has thickened so that it coats a wooden spoon, add the vanilla, stir, remove the pan from the stove, and allow to cool slightly.

While the egg mixture is still warm, pour it over the bananas to cover them. Sprinkle the remaining 2 tablespoons of sugar over all.

Place the pie in the preheated oven and bake 35–40 minutes, or until the egg mixture is firm to the touch. Remove from the oven and cool to room temperature.

TRADE SECRETS FROM A THREE-STAR CHEF

NOTE: *To avoid a mushy bottom crust, always lightly dust the interior of the pie crust with flour before adding the filling.*

DO-AHEAD MISCELLANY

—You may mix the ingredients for the salmon cakes and shape them into patties in the morning. Keep them in the refrigerator, loosely covered with plastic wrap, until ready to sauté.

—Sauté the onions (but do not add the balsamic vinegar) early in the day; keep loosely covered but do not refrigerate.

—The chocolate banana tart holds up well if you make it in the morning. Keep at room temperature, loosely covered, until ready to serve.

NOTE: *The items on this menu do not freeze well.*

8

Blessed Be This Kind of Overindulgence

A PARADOXICAL MENU DESIGNED FOR HEALING

Do certain foods have medicinal properties? Just ask cold sufferers who have sipped chicken soup; they know of food's healing effects. Better yet, look to the French for answers about the curative powers of food: They consume 30 percent more fat and smoke more than Americans do, yet they suffer fewer heart attacks. What's their secret?

If, on November 17, 1991, you watched "60 Minutes" or read the front page of the *New York Times* the next day, you already know the answer to the puzzle of *le paradoxe français:* alcohol, particularly red wine, appears to ward off the nasty effects of a diet loaded with fat. We were excited by the news, but not surprised—if the Frenchman's love affair with rich food and wine makes him happy, why shouldn't it keep him healthy as well?

One of Anne's favorite "healing food" stories also comes from France. She recalls:

"During one of my first visits to Paris, I became friends with a young woman who was experiencing Europe for the very first time. Of course, she was loving every minute of her brief stay, trying to pack in all the glorious sights and attempting to eat and drink everything in sight. For breakfast, it was croissants served with butter and *confiture* and three or four café au laits. For lunch, three or four courses with rich sauces, plus lots of lovely wine. Midafternoon, a chocolate treat with a glass or two of sherry. And for dinner, another three or four sumptuous courses, each served with wine, followed by dessert, cognac, and perhaps an espresso.

"Unfortunately her overindulgence finally caught up with her and one day, quite suddenly, she found herself bedridden with a mysterious illness.

"After a day of suffering she dragged herself to a doctor and told him about the spasmodic pain on the right side of her stomach, and the dull ache in her upper digestive tract. Fully expecting him to reserve a hospital bed and to schedule surgery as well, my friend was dumbstruck when the physician sent her to the pharmacy instead. No, the doctor didn't say Mylanta. He recommended artichoke pills, of course!

"The size of little footballs, the pills had to be sliced in half in order for my friend to chew them, but she ate them religiously, three times a day for the next two days.

"I can't tell you what exactly was wrong with this young woman. What I *do* know, however, is that the artichoke pills seemed to act like a filter for her liver. And they worked like a charm! As the doctor predicted, her condition quickly returned to normal."

NOTE: *Eighteenth-century Europeans considered fresh artichokes a remedy for various ailments. For "those of a phlegmatic or melancholy disposition," noted one French food writer of the period, the "artichaut" was a great elixir. It was also considered an aphrodisiac, and women were forbidden to eat it!**

*Prosper Montagné, Larousse Gastronomique, New York: Crown Publishers, 1961, p. 38.

The artichoke is one of the featured attractions of this menu, which we designed in honor of foods that heal. Of course we've also added a few paradoxical twists of our own. Example: With the artichokes, we're serving hollandaise sauce. Obviously we are not intimidated by those who pooh-pooh the idea of serving anything made with egg yolks and butter. We prefer to take it on faith that the artichoke is our friend, and we trust it will protect us from the delicious poisons of a sinfully rich hollandaise. Besides, throughout the evening we'll be serving lots of red wine—for medicinal purposes, of course. And we also promise to try very hard *not* to enjoy ourselves.

CREATIVE MENU PLANNING 101

Instead of creating menus that feature recipes from only one country or culture, experiment with two, as we did with this chapter's Sino-French dinner. The Master's Chicken from China incorporates beautifully into the European tradition and it gains its rightful place as one of the stars of the meal.

If you have a favorite recipe from your Turkish grandmother, for example, by all means work it into a European-style menu. Really, any *excellent* dish can qualify, as you'll see in Chapter 15, where an extraordinary meatloaf takes centerstage. When something is delicious unto itself, we think it deserves our complete attention.

Artichokes Hollandaise

Are you still clipping off the tips of artichokes before cooking—and rubbing them with lemon so they don't become discolored? Such a waste of time and effort! Solution: Cook the artichokes first, then *clip the tips. It's also easier (and less dangerous!) to clip them once they've been softened by cooking.*

4 to 6	*artichokes, rinsed in cold water, uncut and untrimmed*
1/4	*cup extra-virgin olive oil*
1/4	*teaspoon each salt and pepper*

Place the artichokes in a 4-quart pot (*not* aluminum) and add enough cold water to come halfway up the sides of the artichokes. Add the oil, salt, and pepper. Cover the pot and bring to a boil. Lower the heat and cook until the inner leaves of the artichokes can be easily removed. Remove from the water and let cool. *Do not refrigerate.*

When cool enough to handle, clip off the pointed leaf tips with scissors. With a sharp knife, cut the root end so that the artichoke will stand up on its own.

To serve, place an artichoke in the center of a salad-size plate and spread the leaves attractively. The hollandaise sauce should be served next to the artichoke, either in a small bowl or simply poured on the plate. Serve with a small knife and fork so that your guests can remove the choke and devour the heart.

TIP: *The olive oil added to the water keeps the artichokes supple and imparts a nice glossy look. It's also the reason you can prepare them early in the day without worrying that they'll dry out. They won't.*

Perfect Hollandaise

There will always be those hollandaise aficionados who tell you it should not be made any other way than by hand. Nonsense, we say—as long as there's not a storm brewing outside,* you can make it in your Cuisinart (or blender) with perfect results every time!

9	egg yolks at room temperature†
	Juice from 1/2 lemon
4	*splashes Tabasco sauce*
8	*ounces (2 sticks) melted sweet butter*

Place the egg yolks in a Cuisinart fitted with the steel blade. Add the lemon juice and Tabasco sauce. Start the machine and add the melted butter very slowly through the feed tube until all is incorporated. *Voilà—parfait* every time!

*We haven't the slightest idea why a storm should affect the outcome of a Hollandaise processed in a Cuisinart or blender. Or why, for that matter, turbulent weather destroys soup stocks. We just know that it does.

†Never use a doubtful egg with any odor or discoloration, especially one that is cracked: here is where salmonella can develop.

NOTES ABOUT HOLLANDAISE

—Temperature is everything. The eggs *must* be room temperature or they will not bind with the butter. The butter *must* be warm but not hot, or it will reject—or cook—the eggs. How to know when the butter is ready: After you've turned off the flame and the butter has stopped bubbling, it's ready to pour.

—Always use a 2-ounce ladle for pouring the melted butter into the feed tube; it's much easier than juggling a saucepan and so much more efficient than transferring the butter to a measuring cup first and then pouring it into the tube. (A small ladle is also great for basting all types of food, for pouring small portions of sauce onto individual servings, and simply for *tasting* things—gravies, soups, stocks, etc.)

—Hollandaise should never be poured over an artichoke; it must be served on the side, either on the plate that holds the artichoke or in a small dish.

—There's little reason to fear hollandaise on the grounds that it's "bad" for you. With most dishes we can think of, the amount served is quite modest: in fact, if you've had a quarter-cup of it, you've had a lot. We also suspect that worrying is more deleterious to our bodies than a few tablespoons of hollandaise!

—Hollandaise is the mother of many other sauces. Add whipped cream and you have a mousseline a.k.a. chantilly; work in shallots, tarragon, and white wine and you've done a béarnaise; substitute blood-orange juice and rind for the lemon and you've created a Maltaise—just to name a few. All can be prepared flawlessly in the Cuisinart or blender, as long as the temperature rules are followed.

The Master's Chicken

It is fascinating that the Chinese, who use an incredible amount of salty soy sauce, do not suffer from high blood pressure. Perhaps this paradox occurs because the national food of China happens to be rice (which, by the way, is often recommended for patients who suffer from hypertension). Though it hasn't been scientifically documented, it does seem quite clear that all of us should be striving to maintain some sort of delicate gastronomic balance—of positives and negatives—in every meal we eat.

The more you contemplate this "yin-yang" nature of food, the more you'll want to experiment with healing combinations in every menu. Take our main course, for example: chicken prepared in a soy sauce–based mixture, served with Perfect Rice. The two offset, yet complement, each other. Plus, they're absolutely delicious and never fail to wow dinner guests. Don't tell anyone how easy this meal is to prepare—just let them marvel at your culinary skill!

2	cups Kikkoman soy sauce
4	cups cold water
One	1-inch piece of fresh ginger, peeled and cut into chunks
2	whole star anise or 1 1/2 tablespoons Pernod
One	4-pound whole chicken, washed and patted dry
2	tablespoons sugar
	Sesame oil, for brushing chicken
Optional:	lettuce leaves or chopped scallions, for garnish

NOTE: *For six guests, use one 4-pound whole chicken plus two bone-in breasts with skin left on.*

Into a 2 1/2-quart pot, pour the soy sauce and water and add the ginger and the star anise (or Pernod). Bring to a boil. Add the chicken, breast side down. Cover the pot and boil for

(Continued)

exactly 20 minutes. With the heat still on high, uncover the pot and turn the chicken breast side up. Add the sugar, cover again, and boil for *exactly* 20 minutes more. *Do not peek.* Leave the cover on and let the chicken rest in the pot for two hours.

NOTE: *Do not let the chicken sit in the sauce for more than a total of 2 hours 40 minutes. See box, page 87.*

When ready to serve, remove the chicken and place it on a cutting board. With a sharp knife, cut the meat off the bone and slice into bite-size pieces. Brush each piece *lightly* with sesame oil. If you wish, line a platter with lettuce leaves and place the chicken pieces attractively on top. Or place the chicken pieces on your platter and sprinkle it with chopped scallions.

VARIATION: *Since you'll have a lot of sauce left over from this recipe, try it on shrimp, pork, swordfish, or any firm-fleshed fish. It works as a marinade and is particularly delicious when brushed on grilled dishes. (Do not use it on beef, though; a fatty taste will result.) After the sauce has cooled, defat it, put it into a glass jar, and cover tightly. Kept refrigerated, it will last for weeks.*

TRADE SECRETS FROM A THREE-STAR CHEF

A RUBBER CHICKEN STORY

Upon tasting The Master's Chicken for the first time, a friend begged for the recipe when he learned how easy it is to prepare. He doesn't like to cook, but feels obliged to give a dinner party from time to time, and this sounded like the answer to his culinary prayers.

In his zeal to "get it over with," however, he decided to prepare the dish early in the day—at 8 o'clock on the morning of his party to be exact. So there the bird sat, soaking in a soy sauce-based marinade, for about 12 hours. (Had we known this, we might not have shown up for dinner that night. And we certainly would have tried to prevent him from giving *us* the "credit" for the recipe in front of all his guests!)

As we watched our fellow guests take their first bites, we knew something had gone awry. Usually cheerful people began frowning, normally boisterous people grew quiet. Everyone, to a person, groped for the water pitcher. When we took a bite, we knew in a moment what had gone wrong: Not only had the salt utterly permeated the meat, it had begun to *preserve* it as well. The result: the most rubbery, inedible chicken ever served outside a political banquet or military mess hall.

Let this be a lesson. When we say 2 hours and 40 minutes total time for The Master's Chicken, we mean it!

Perfect Rice

If you follow the directions exactly, *this rice really will be perfect. (See box before you begin.)*

6   *cups cold water*

3   *cups long grain white rice (preferably Uncle Ben's Converted)*

Bring the water to a boil in a *covered* 2 1/2-quart heavy saucepan. Add the rice. Bring to a boil again, then turn down the heat to very low and cover again. Cook for approximately 20 minutes, or until all the liquid has evaporated. (See box about rice.)

Baby Peas in the French Method

On the subject of petit pois, no one has been more eloquent than Madame de Maintenon, who, in 1696, told the Cardinal of Noailles, "The anticipation of eating them, the pleasure of having eaten them, the joy of eating them again are the three subjects that our princes have been discussing for four days....It has become a fashion—indeed, a passion."*

We're passionate for peas, too, especially in this recipe, which transforms a rather ordinary vegetable into a creation that is absolutely sublime. We hope you'll serve them as a separate course. After all, shouldn't a food so wonderful—and so healthy—have centerstage all to itself?

1/2	cup chicken stock, preferably homemade
6	tablespoons sweet butter
Three	10-ounce packages of frozen tiny or baby peas, defrosted
1	head Boston lettuce, cut into four wedges
1	large Vidalia or sweet white onion, peeled and cut into 4 wedges
1 1/2	tablespoons sugar
1/2	teaspoon salt
1/2	teaspoon pepper

Bring the chicken stock and butter to a boil in a 3 1/2-quart saucepan. Add the peas and toss with the liquid. Add the lettuce, onions, sugar, salt, and pepper and toss again. Cover the saucepan and turn the heat down to low. Cook for 8 minutes. Uncover and turn the heat up to boil off the remaining liquid; stir occasionally.

Serve as a separate course in a small soup bowl *with a spoon.*

*Larousse Gastronomique, p. 781.

IN FRANCE . . .

. . . classical purists who prepare peas in the French method will say that you must tie your lettuce with string so it won't fall apart during cooking, and that you should remove both lettuce and onion before serving. What an insane idea—all the ingredients are so delicious!

Applesauce Muffins with Hot Honey-Walnut Sauce

Because of the wholesome ingredients, you'll want to call this health food. But please don't.

PREHEAT THE OVEN TO 425°.
YIELD: 12 MUFFINS

For the muffins:

	Vegetable cooking spray
1 1/4	cups all-purpose flour
1 1/4	cups "quick" rolled oats
1/4	cup light brown sugar, firmly packed
1	tablespoon baking powder
1/4	teaspoon baking soda
1/4	teaspoon salt
1	teaspoon cinnamon
1	teaspoon nutmeg
1/8	teaspoon ground cloves
1	egg
3/4	cup milk
3	tablespoons vegetable oil
1	cup applesauce

Lightly spray 12 nonstick muffin cups with vegetable spray.

In a medium bowl, mix together all the dry ingredients. In a large bowl, combine the egg, milk, oil, and applesauce and mix well. Just before ready to bake, pour the liquid mixture into the dry mixture and fold them together until just mixed. (The batter will look lumpy.) Fill the muffin cups 2/3 full and bake for 15–20 minutes. When done, the muffins will be golden-brown and firm but slightly moist to the touch. A toothpick inserted in the center will come out clean.

For the sauce:

6	tablespoons honey
3	tablespoons melted sweet butter
1/4	cup chopped walnuts

Heat the honey and butter together in a sauté pan until bubbly, then add the walnuts. Remove from the heat and drizzle 1–2 teaspoons over each muffin. Serve immediately.

BLESSED BE THIS KIND OF OVERINDULGENCE

DO-AHEAD MISCELLANY

—You may boil the artichokes 2–3 hours in advance. Remove them from the water and cool. Do not refrigerate.
—Although the actual blending of the hollandaise sauce must be done at the last minute, you can certainly assemble a line-up of small dishes an hour or so beforehand and fill one with the egg yolks (at room temperature, but see †NOTE, page 83), and another with the lemon juice. You may also melt your butter in advance, but make sure you reheat it slowly and carefully just before adding it to the egg yolks or it will not bind properly.
—The Master's Chicken is a do-ahead recipe already, since the chicken spends *exactly* 2 hours and 40 minutes cooking in its liquid. But remember, bad things will happen if you extend the time—see box for a cautionary tale.
—The petit pois should be thoroughly defrosted in advance—take them out of the freezer a couple of hours before serving time.
—You may bake the muffins early in the day, but 5 minutes after removing them from the oven, cover them *lightly* with a clean dish towel or table napkin. This will keep them moist. After they've cooled completely (as always, do not refrigerate), pop them in a plastic bag and leave the end open; this keeps them from drying out but also allows enough air circulation so that they don't "sweat." Reheat briefly before serving.

NOTE: *The muffins freeze well if you cool them completely and wrap well in plastic wrap. Other items on this menu do not freeze well.*

9

Remembrance of Bistros Past

WITH THE RIGHT FOOD, AMBIENCE, AND ATTITUDE, YOU CAN RELIVE THOSE DAYS OF YESTERYEAR

*W*hile we were preparing this chapter, we learned that the bistros of France are dying out, strangled by Burger Kings and McDonald's. A copy of *Time* arrived with a quick take on the bad news: "Will the Hemingways, the Sartres and the Picassos of the next century debate ideas while dining out on le hamburger and le Coca-Cola? The scenario is hardly far fetched," the correspondent warned. "For on street corners of Paris, and in provincial cities from Lille to Lourdes, le fast food is muscling out bistros at a dizzying rate."

The details make one's head spin. It seems that at the turn of the century, France boasted 300,000 cafés for its 38 million inhabitants; today, you'll find only 62,000 for 58 million. Most astonishing: In the past decade alone, bistros have vanished at the rate of 3,500 a year. "Each time a café closes, a little bit of liberty and democracy disappears," mused a seventy-one-year-old bistro owner to *Time*. From the window of his café, Le Petit Poucet, this fellow must endure the sight of potential customers flocking to Le Quick, a fast-food joint just footsteps away.

It's a sad state of affairs for the French, not to mention for future generations of Americans, who might never have the chance to rest an elbow on le zinc and savor a shot of pastis after

Chilled Champagne Served with Herb-Cheese Puff Pastries

Choucroute Garni with Carrots and Steamed Potatoes

Kirsch Soufflé

SERVES 4–6

a meal. Alas, lamenting the situation will not change things, but one can certainly fight back in a small and personal way: that is, by creating one's own bistro evening at home for friends and family. One can, at least, keep the Gallic spirit alive!

If you've never been to a French bistro (and if you've been to one on American turf, then you still haven't), you've missed out on a special restaurant experience that melds warmth, coziness, a feeling of family, and even of romance, with down-to-earth comfort foods such as hearty, bubbling cassoulets, sizzling sausages, whole chicken and 40 cloves of garlic, crusty peasant breads, creamy flans, and tangy plum tarts.

A real bistro is a let-your-hair-down kind of place, where the dress is *très* casual, the wine need not be expensive, and all the friends are good ones. That's why it's the perfect ambience for an intimate dinner party for four to six.

To help you create the kind of atmosphere you might find in a Paris bistro, we offer the following ideas. The suggestions may not be for everyone, but all of them are fun—which is precisely what your bistro evening should be. Here goes:

—Measure your dining room table, then go to your charcuterie and beg for some free butcher paper. You'll use this for a table cloth. If you're feeling really daring, put some crayons on the table and encourage guests to scribble freely; this will approximate the look of a bistro table from the fifties and sixties, when a maître d' might have written your order on the paper, for your waiter to glance at on his way to the kitchen.

—This is an evening when you can get away with vin ordinaire—a.k.a. decent jug wine. Buy lots of it—preferably red, because it's so good for you—and then serve it in jelly glasses à la Bonne Maman. Keep the jug on the table at all times—i.e., don't be phony and pour the wine into a carafe to conceal how little you've spent. If things are going the way they should, nobody will care. (By the way, since you're going to save a bundle on the wine, live it up and serve a little champagne with your appetizer. So French!)

—Atmosphere is everything. The smell of a bistro is

so wonderful: a pleasant mixture of goose fat and diesel exhaust and the scent of Gauloise cigarettes. But that's difficult to duplicate at home. So concentrate instead on the lighting—too much will destroy the mood. Use your dimmer switch. Then, here and there, place votive candles in stout little holders so that the room looks cozy and warm. Never use a scented candle in this or any other room where food is served. Can you imagine the assault on the olfactory nerves when Forest Pine collides with pork and sauerkraut? (Oh, one more thing: Please don't stick candles in old Chianti bottles drizzled with wax. That's something the Italians used to do before they got so busy making 300,000 varieties of pasta.)

—Of course you'll want fresh flowers, but this is not the evening for velvet-black orchids and skinny willow branches. Pick simple, colorful flowers from the garden—or buy them from your florist—then literally *grab* a bunch and *stuff* it in an old glass jar filled with water. The look you want to achieve isn't sloppy or careless, it's simply unpretentious and says "I've been here for a while."

—You must have music, preferably the kind that breaks the heart. If you know somebody who can play the accordion, don't invite him. Instead, choose Josephine Baker or Edith Piaf—her "I Regret Nothing" is so moving—or Montand, even Aznavour if that's all you have.

—If you're a person who likes to do color themes, your best bet for tonight is the Tri-Colour, which refers to the French flag of blue, white, and red. Blue napkins on your white tablecloth with red flowers would be nice, perhaps flanked on one side by a pack of Gitanes *filtre* cigarettes in the blue and white box. But whatever you do, don't use anything with red and white checks. That's Italian, *chérie,* and trite besides.

As for the meal itself, both the start and the finish are light and airy, the perfect accompaniments to a classic Choucroute Garni. It's completely unpretentious and soul-satisfying—a hearty dish for an evening when *le cocooning* with close friends is all you want to do.

...does not come from that familiar bright green can you may have used as a kid. (Unfortunately, that horrid stuff is still available—and chock-full of preservatives and fillers that taste like sawdust). For incomparable flavor, buy *Parmigiano,* available grated or in wedges.

Herb-Cheese Puff Pastries

These elegant puff pastry sticks are a splendid way to start a meal with a main course as filling as choucroute garni. If you're feeling flush, serve them with champagne for a special treat.

PREHEAT THE OVEN TO 400°.

One	*8 × 12 sheet puff pastry*
1/4	*cup grated Parmesan cheese, plus additional for sprinkling*
3	*tablespoons dried herbs of your choice*
Optional:	*dash of cayenne*

Remove the pastry from its package and lay it flat on a lightly floured cutting board or other "portable" surface that will fit inside your refrigerator. (If the dough is frozen, allow it to come to room temperature—check package instructions for specifics.)

Sprinkle the dough with the cheese and herbs and, if you wish, the cayenne. Fold the pastry in half, pat it gently to seal the edges. Then, with a rolling pin, roll out the dough to 1/4 inch thick. Refrigerate for 20 minutes.

Remove the pastry from the refrigerator and, with a sharp knife, slice it into strips approximately 1/2 inch wide. With your hands, twist each strip into a corkscrew shape and place them on an ungreased baking sheet.

Bake in the preheated oven for 12–15 minutes or until golden brown. Remove from the oven and sprinkle with additional grated Parmesan cheese while still warm. Allow to cool but do not refrigerate.

Serve at room temperature.

PUFF PASTRY TIPS

—Don't overwork the dough, and make sure you keep it chilled: puff pastry is loaded with butter, which will melt if handled too much. NOTE: If, at any point in the recipe, you feel the dough becoming greasy or too soft, just pop it in the refrigerator for 10 minutes to allow the butter to firm up.

—Slicing dough is easier if you keep a little flour on the sharp edge of the knife. Pour about 1/4 cupful of flour on your work surface, then insert the cutting edge of your knife into it before making each slice.

—If you're new to the wonders of puff pastry and are unsure about the consistency of the dough after you shape the corkscrews, place them in the refrigerator for 10 minutes before baking.

JUNIPER VS. GIN

When a hint of gin is called for in a recipe, you can either pour in the spirits or add juniper berries, which are used in the making of gin and give the liquor its distinctive aroma. Don't use both or the result will be overpowering.

THE SECRETS OF SIMMERING

If you want the pork in the choucroute to be as tender as possible, you must keep your pot at the simmer, or as the French say, *mijoter*. Sounds easy, but if you can't get a low enough flame on your stove, you may end up boiling—and toughening—the meat. A quick and inexpensive solution: Buy a heat deflector. It sits on top of your burner (and under your pan) and spreads the heat evenly. Cost: under $4.00.

Choucroute Garni with Carrots and Steamed Potatoes

The Alsace region is known for its pork and its sauerkraut, and this dish is a great showcase for both. It's really easy to make—much of it is simply a matter of adding ingredients to the pot.

PREHEAT THE OVEN TO 350°.

Four	12-ounce packages sauerkraut
2	large onions, cut into 1-inch pieces
4	tablespoons sweet butter
2	large carrots, peeled and cut into 1-inch pieces
1/4	pound bacon, cut into 1-inch pieces
2	cups white wine
1/4	cup gin or 10 juniper berries (not both: see box)
1	cup beef broth, preferably College Inn
	A bouquet garni (see box, page 99)
2	pounds pork loin roast
3	tablespoons vegetable oil
One	16-ounce kielbasa
1	pound bratwurst or other pork sausage
4–6	Idaho or russet potatoes, steamed or boiled separately

Wash the sauerkraut in at least 3 changes of water, or until the brine is almost gone. Wring out the water and spread the sauerkraut evenly on paper toweling. Set aside.

In a 3 1/2-quart casserole, sauté the onions in butter for 3 minutes. Add the carrots and sauté for 5 minutes until crisp-tender. Add the bacon and sauté until lightly browned. Add the sauerkraut and toss with the cooked ingredients. Add the wine,

TRADE SECRETS FROM A THREE-STAR CHEF

gin, broth, and bouquet garni and toss again. Continue to simmer on low.

In a separate sauté pan, brown the pork loin in vegetable oil. Then bury it in the sauerkraut, put the casserole in the preheated oven, covered, and cook for 2 1/2 hours.

When the pork roast is cooked through, bury the kielbasa and the remaining pork ingredients in the sauerkraut, making sure you have pricked the casings on the sausages. Cook for one more hour.

NOTE: *During the last half-hour of cooking the choucroute, boil or steam the potatoes in a separate pot. They needn't be peeled, but should be cut into quarters just before serving.*

Serve the choucroute steaming hot, with Dijon mustard on the side. (See box below for presentation ideas.)

PORK PICKS

Almost any pork product can be used in the Choucroute Garni. Here are some suggestions:

Pork loin, rump, shoulder, spareribs, chops; sausage, smoked ham, kielbasa, bratwurst, frankfurters.

NOTE: *If you use pork tenderloin, allow it to cook only 30 minutes buried in the sauerkraut. Follow the times specified in the recipe for other types of pork*

PRESENTATION FOR CHOUCROUTE

On a very large platter, arrange all the pork in the center, surround it with sauerkraut, then alternate carrots and potatoes in an outside border. The occasional sprig of parsley looks attractive amid the vegetables.

Or keep the sauerkraut and vegetables separate, arranged attractively on a platter. On another platter, arrange the pork in a formal composition.

SHOULD YOU DROP A FAGGOT INTO YOUR SAUCE?

Yes! But these days, you better call it by its other name: A *bouquet garni,* a wonderful way to infuse sauces, soups, or stews with a subtle herb flavor. You can buy *bouquets garnis* in specialty stores, but they're fun and inexpensive to make at home. Here's how: In the center of a 6-inch-square piece of cheesecloth, place 1 teaspoon each dried thyme, parsley, chervil, plus 3 peppercorns and 1 clove. (A few tablespoons of *herbes de Provence* work well, too.) Then fold up the cloth so it looks like a little bag and tie it tightly with string. A *bouquet garni* should be removed from the liquid and discarded after use.

THE EGG AND YOU

Egg whites kept at *room temperature* (about 70°) and beaten for 3 to 5 minutes will produce the most billowy soufflé.

A REMINDER ABOUT THE "RIBBON STAGE"

When beating together eggs and sugar over heat, this stage occurs when the two ingredients have been sufficiently mixed—and incorporated with enough air. When you pour the mixture from a wooden spoon, a wide "ribbon" of liquid should fall from it. If you pour and get a thin stream of liquid, keep beating.

SERVING AFTER-DINNER COFFEE?

Try adding a tablespoonful of ground chocolate to the top of the coffee in the pot before you add boiling water. It adds a richness and depth, yet it doesn't really taste chocolatey. (This technique works best with coffee that's made in a filter-type pot, such as Melitta.)

Kirsch Soufflé

This airy dessert is a heavenly way to enjoy the eau-de-vie known as kirsch.

PREHEAT THE OVEN TO 400°.

	Ice cubes in a metal bowl large enough to accommodate your saucepan
2/3	*cup sugar*
8	*egg yolks*
1/2	*cup kirsch*
1/4	*cup finely crushed vanilla wafers*
10	*egg whites*
	Dash of cream of tartar
	Confectioner's sugar for dusting

Have ready the bowl full of ice cubes. (You will be nestling your saucepan in it to stop the egg mixture from cooking.) Butter the bottom of an 8-inch soufflé dish.

Combine the sugar and egg yolks in a medium saucepan over a very low flame. Using an electric mixer, beat the sugar and yolks together until their consistency reaches the "ribbon stage" (see box). Add the kirsch, stir well to blend, then remove the pan from heat and place in the bowl of ice cubes. Continue to beat until the mixture is cool. Fold in the vanilla wafers and set aside.

In a large mixing bowl (preferably copper), beat the egg whites and the cream of tartar with an electric mixer until stiff but not dry.

With a spatula, gently fold the egg yolk mixture into the whites, then scoop into the prepared soufflé dish. Bake for about 25 minutes, or until the top is golden brown.

Dust with confectioner's sugar and serve immediately, with a small glass of kirsch on the side (or if you prefer, a demitasse of steaming hot espresso).

DO-AHEAD MISCELLANY

—Put the champagne (or wine) on its side in the refrigerator in the morning—it should be between 35° and 40° to be properly chilled.

—The puff pastries can be made a day in advance. Carefully place them in a tin with a tight-fitting lid—or wrap them in parchment paper.

—You will, perforce, begin the choucroute several hours in advance. (Don't try to make this a day ahead—the results are disappointing.)

—Soufflés are last-minute productions. But do remember to remove the eggs from the refrigerator in the morning so they'll be at room temperature.

NOTE: *The items on this menu do not freeze well.*

10

The Tao of Chinese Cooking

HOW TO CREATE A MEAL THAT'S A MYSTICAL EXPERIENCE

*I*t has been said that when you are bitten by the "restaurant bug," you either die of stupidity, or you lose all your money and *then* die of stupidity. It seems, therefore, somewhat miraculous that Anne is still alive today, with enough brain cells intact to reconstruct the story of why and how, in the mid-seventies, she opened a Chinese restaurant on the North Fork of Long Island:

"It wasn't that I knew more about this type of food than other Americans, or that I knew anything about it at all—I didn't. I was compelled to open this restaurant for two reasons: because I love *real* Chinese food, and because there were no restaurants of its kind, or caliber, in the area.

"Everyone was excited when my partners and I decided to buy the old, run-down garage we would eventually transform into one of the very first upscale Chinese restaurants on the East End. Excitement grew with every dollar we spent—around $222 billion as I recall—and with every elegant touch: wineglasses on the tables, white linen tablecloths, fresh flowers every day, not to mention an incredible Oriental garden complete with plants and Buddhas and temples and spouting fountains. It really was a gorgeous place, and in the entire history of the world, I think it was the first and only Chinese restaurant ever to have a fabulous bar that served fabulous drinks.

"We needed just the right name for our restaurant, so we had a contest among all our friends. You cannot imagine (and I dare not repeat) some of the names that were submitted! Eventually, the winning entry came from a Shelter Island couple who'd been influential in the placement of Vietnamese families in America. Since they knew I'd always wanted a French country inn, they came up with a combination of China plus America and gave it a French pronunciation. The result was Chinam.

"We hired a young man named Alexander Wong to be our chef. From him, I learned everything I ever knew—or ever will know—about food. He was a true genius: He could produce a Chinese—or authentic French—meal on the spot without batting an eye. He had a sense of humor, too; he always wore a baseball cap askew on his head—and this was long before anybody had ever heard of Wolfgang Puck.

"Alexander was eccentric and completely whacko, but I absolutely adored him. Because of his great talent, within a mere six months Chinam had received its three stars from the *New York Times*."

In this chapter, you will learn some of the secrets of authentic Chinese cooking that Alexander Wong taught Anne during his stint at Chinam. And perhaps to your own astonishment, you will discover you, too, can create a meal that will be a mystical experience. The progression of the food will be in tune with your body, and the ingredients will balance the yin with the yang. Perhaps most important, we hope a realization will occur among you and your guests: At last you will understand *why,* long after Western man has murdered himself in myriad ways, the Chinese will still be on the planet. Through their food and the way it's prepared and served, you'll get a glimpse of how intelligently they live.

Peking Scallion Noodles

The Chinese invented pasta, so it's no wonder they have developed the most wonderful pasta dishes of all the cuisines. This first course is more than just beautiful to look at—it's positively addictive and couldn't be simpler to make.

8–12	ounces good-quality spaghetti
1	teaspoon sesame oil
1	cup creamy peanut butter
1 1/2	cups hot tea, brewed very strong
2	tablespoons soy sauce
1	tablespoon honey
2	cloves garlic, minced
	Dash of Mongolian fire oil (or Tabasco)
2–4	scallions, cleaned, trimmed, and cut in 2-inch pieces (including green part), for garnish

Prepare the spaghetti "al dente" according to package directions. Rinse and refresh it with cold water to stop the cooking, then drain and toss with the sesame oil. Set aside.

Thin out the peanut butter with the tea until it is the consistency of mayonnaise. Combine the peanut butter with the remaining ingredients (except the scallions) in a medium saucepan and heat until melted. Set aside.

Just before serving, toss the noodles with peanut sauce* and place on a large platter. Sprinkle artfully with the scallions and serve at room temperature.

---

*Less is more: Use just enough peanut sauce to cover noodles. Leftover sauce lasts for months in the refrigerator.

Many home cooks shy away from Chinese cooking because the recipes often require *many* ingredients—in small amounts, chopped or minced—to be added in a specific order. The best way to control the chaos: place the prepared ingredients in "monkey bowls," small (half-cup) dishes that can be arranged in assembly line fashion. Use teacups, small jars, saucers, lids—whatever you have around the house.

A friend had a tough time with the Mahogany Duck recipe. She tried it twice and claimed it "didn't work"— each time the duck was greasy and not crisp. After strenuous cross-questioning, we discovered the problem:

Knowing how much oil would drip from the duck during roasting—and fearing it would be baked onto her roasting pan, she decided to add water to the bottom of the pan so that cleanup would be easier. Good intentions, bad result: *Steamed* duck!

If you're worried about cleanup, line your pan with parchment paper.

Mahogany Duck

This is one of the dishes from Chinam that became a popular favorite at The Station. It tastes "authentic" even though the preparation has been updated for twentieth-century cooks (see box).

PREHEAT THE OVEN TO 350°.

One	4–5-pound fresh or thoroughly defrosted duck
2	cloves garlic, peeled but left whole
One	1-inch piece fresh ginger, peeled, left whole
1	cup soy sauce, preferably Kikkoman
1/2	cup honey
1/4	cup dry vermouth
	Sprigs of cilantro, for garnish

Rinse the duck with cold water and pat dry inside and out. With the tines of a fork, or the point of a very sharp knife, prick the duck flesh all over—about 8–10 times. Place the garlic and ginger inside the cavity.

Mix the soy sauce, honey, and vermouth until thoroughly blended, then brush all over the duck. Reserve any extra sauce.

Place the duck on a rack in a large roasting pan, breast side up, and roast for 1 1/2 hours. Remove from the oven and let rest for 10–15 minutes. Cut the duck into 6–8 pieces, place on a baking sheet, and set aside.

Just before serving, preheat the broiler. Brush each piece of duck with additional sauce, then place under the broiler until the skin browns and crisps—about 5–6 minutes. *Watch carefully to avoid burning.* Serve immediately on a large platter, garnished, if you wish, with sprigs of cilantro (Chinese parsley).

WONG'S ANCIENT CHINESE SECRETS

When preparing an authentic Chinese recipe, do not stray from the order in which the ingredients are given—there are perfectly logical reasons for the order, including:

1. It is based on the texture of the food and the required cooking time; if you change the order, something will either burn or be undercooked. If added too early in the sequence, for example, sugar will caramelize and change the taste and texture of the dish.
2. The Oriental balance of the yin and the yang, the feminine and the masculine, the anima and the animus, must be maintained. Balance may be achieved within a menu (we start with sweet and end with sour), or within a recipe: the garlic-ginger-sugar trio found in the fried rice mellows the onion that came before, and enlivens the bland water chestnuts and bamboo shoots that follow. The result? Perfect harmony.

THE LAST STRAW

How many ways are there to achieve a crisp duck? If memory serves, we've seen a number of techniques over the years, mentioned in cookbooks we've long since thrown away. Favorite recollections: "Insert straw beneath skin and blow..." (You picture Lauren Bacall, don't you?) And how about: "Hang bird, head down, from ceiling for 48 hours." All-time favorite: "Now take your bicycle pump and insert tubing under skin and with your foot, work the pump..." We wonder: Is anybody out there still using these arcane techniques?

When cooking in the Chinese tradition, you *will* get the best results from a wok (vs. a sauté pan). Look for one made of lightweight tin or aluminum with a long heat-proof handle. If you pay more than $25, you're being ripped off.

To "season" a wok, heat it on medium high, add kosher salt until the wok is half full, then "cook" for half an hour. Remove and discard the salt. Apply a thin coating of peanut oil after each use.

Never, *ever* use butter in a wok. It simply is *not* done.

What about an electric wok? Use it as a nut bowl or planter.

Yung Chow Rice

This recipe will rival the fried rice at your favorite Chinese restaurant. It's an intricate and complex dish, one that requires strict discipline to make properly. "Do not allow your ego to interfere," Alex Wong always preached. "The order of ingredients must not be changed."

4–5	tablespoons peanut oil
1	stalk celery, finely chopped
1	small onion, finely chopped
1	teaspoon minced garlic
1	teaspoon minced fresh ginger
1	teaspoon sugar
One	6-ounce can water chestnuts, drained and finely chopped
One	6-ounce can bamboo shoots, drained and finely chopped
1	cup finely chopped cooked shrimp (or one 8-ounce can tiny shrimp, drained and rinsed)
2	tablespoons oyster sauce
2	tablespoons mild soy sauce
5	cups cooked white rice (see box, page 109)
1	egg, mixed well, stir-fried, and cut into thin strips (see box, page 109)
1/2	cup frozen peas, defrosted
Optional:	1/2 cup slivered almonds, roasted and lightly salted

Heat a wok or 12-inch sauté pan on medium-high, and when a sprinkling of water skips across it, add 2 tablespoons of the oil and turn the pan to coat evenly. Add the celery and stir-fry for 3 minutes, then add the onion, garlic, ginger, and sugar and stir-fry for 1 more minute. Add the water chestnuts, bamboo shoots, and shrimp and fry for another minute. Add oyster and soy sauces and mix well. Remove all ingredients from the wok and set aside.

Wipe the wok clean with paper towels, then heat up again and add 2 more tablespoons of oil. Add the cooked rice a cup at a time, stirring briskly and constantly. Add the previously cooked ingredients to the rice and stir until well mixed. Remove from the heat. Add the egg strips and peas, and toss.

Serve immediately in an attractive bowl, sprinkled, if you wish, with slivered almonds.

FRIED RICE TRICKS OF THE TRADE

We have a friend who buys fried rice from his favorite restaurant, adds a few ingredients of his own, and then takes *all* the credit for the dish. But why spend that kind of money when you can make your own *superior* fried rice? Remember these tricks:

—Always cook the rice a day (or more) in advance. Keep chilled until ready to fry and then, with a fork, fluff gently to separate before plunging it into the oil.
—Rice must be cooked separately, then added to other (cooked) ingredients in the final phase of preparation. Otherwise, the moisture from the other ingredients will draw the starch from the rice, and the result will be mush.
—All meat and vegetable additions should be approximately the same size so they cook evenly.
—To prevent sticking, always heat the wok (or sauté pan) first, then add the oil.
—The oil must be hot—at least 365°, or bubbling but not smoking. (Use the foolproof chopstick technique described on page 12.)

FRESH VS. JAR GINGER

No contest here. *Always* use fresh ginger! The stuff in the jar has virtually no taste or texture, having been soaked in preservative for God knows how long.

Fresh ginger will keep for weeks in a cool, dry place. If you're a refrigerator fanatic, place the ginger anywhere *except* the vegetable drawer, which will turn it to slime in a matter of days.

HOW TO WOK-FRY AN EGG

In a small bowl, whisk one egg until completely mixed, and set aside.

Heat the wok on medium high, then add 1 teaspoon peanut oil and rotate the wok to coat evenly. Pour in the egg and rotate the wok until the egg spreads all along the bottom and as far up the sides as possible. After 20–30 seconds, turn the egg with a spatula, cook a few seconds more, and remove from the wok. Place on paper toweling until cool, then cut into thin slices.

NOTE: *If you use a 12-inch sauté pan, the egg will not reach the sides of the pan.*

Dessert Soup

This is a savory soup, so it may seem an unexpected finish. But when you consider the sweetness of the previous three courses, you'll find it an absolutely appropriate and balanced *end to the meal.*

6	cups chicken stock, preferably homemade (see recipe, page 111)
1/2	cup water chestnuts, sliced
1	teaspoon minced fresh ginger
1	cup julienned snow pea pods (strings removed)
1	cup mushrooms, sliced
1/2	cup thinly sliced cucumber rounds, peeled and deseeded
1	tablespoon sesame oil
1	tablespoon soy sauce, preferably Kikkoman
	Salt if necessary
2	tablespoons chopped scallions

Bring the stock to a boil. Add the water chestnuts, ginger, snow peas, and mushrooms. Lower the heat and simmer 10 minutes. Add the cucumber and bring back to a boil for 2 minutes. Add the sesame oil and soy sauce, stir, and remove from the heat. Taste *first,* then adjust the seasoning, adding salt if necessary.

Serve hot, in individual bowls, with a sprinkling of scallions.

TRADE SECRETS FROM A THREE-STAR CHEF

Chinese Chicken Stock

There are countless recipes for chicken stock, but we think this one works best when used in Oriental dishes such as the dessert soup.

3	pounds chicken backs and necks
One	1/2-inch slice fresh ginger
1	tablespoon salt
8	cups cold water

Combine all ingredients in a large stock pot. Bring to a boil, then lower the heat to a simmer. Cover the pot and cook slowly for 3 hours. Using cheesecloth or a sieve, strain the liquid into a clean pot. Let it cool and degrease. Reserve enough for the dessert soup recipe above, and freeze the rest.

NOTE: *If you must use canned chicken stock, choose one that says "low sodium," and then be prepared to add additional cold water to further subdue the taste.*

TIP: *What can you do with extra stock? Make "flavor cubes": In a medium saucepan, heat 2 extra cups of stock on medium-high and reduce to 1 1/2 cups. Remove from the heat and allow to cool. Pour the reduced stock into an ice cube tray and freeze. Use a cube or two whenever you want to add depth and interest to a soup or a Chinese sauce.*

COLD WATER REMINDER

Don't forget always to use cold water when cooking, even if the recipe requires you to heat it (as in the Basic Chicken Stock here). Cold water is purer—and tastes better—than hot tap water, which is full of sediment from your hot water heater.

DO-AHEAD MISCELLANY

—The peanut sauce can be made weeks ahead. The spaghetti can be made in the morning as long as it's tossed with sesame oil. Keep it covered at room temperature.

—The Mahogany Duck can be prepared several hours in advance; keep it *lightly* covered at room temperature. The final application of sauce and broiler-finishing must be done just before serving.

—The rice *must* be cooked the day before. All the other ingredients can be assembled, added, and cooked up to a day in advance. (Keep lightly covered in the refrigerator.) Reheat with 1 tablespoon peanut oil on high and stir-fry rapidly until hot.

—If you wish to make the Dessert Soup up to a day in advance, do not add any salt after cooking. The soy in the soup will strengthen by the hour and its saltiness—plus that in the chicken stock—may preclude the addition of salt. When you reheat the soup, taste it first, then adjust the seasoning.

NOTE: *The items on this menu do not freeze well.*

TRADE SECRETS FROM A THREE-STAR CHEF

11

And Now for Something Completely Different

HORS D'OEUVRES VARIES
AND NOTHING BUT

So far in this book, we've encouraged you to throw convention to the wind and adopt the European way of eating. For some, that may be enough to ask. The rest of you daring souls who don't mind going one step beyond, we now ask to forget—temporarily—about the Euro-style and instead, take a deep breath and dabble in the downright bizarre. Herewith, a meal comprised only of beautiful appetizers!

The Italians would call it *antipasti,* but our version, known as *hors d'oeuvres varies,* bears no resemblance to its Italian counterpart. As you may know, the American version of antipasti is utterly dull—everything tastes the same because it's all drenched in olive oil, from the slab of salami and the handful of garbanzo beans to the mushy hot pepper, soggy artichoke heart, overly salty olives, and canned tuna fish.

In contrast, these *hors d'oeuvres varies* provide guests with a gastronomic tour de force—each item on the menu is a special little meal all by itself. Nothing tastes like anything else. Each item has its own personality. That's why, at another time, you'll want to serve one select item as a first or second course with an entirely different meal. That's also why we think this menu should be served in separate, dramatic courses—we wouldn't dream of hiding these distinctive delights on a cluttered platter!

Herbed Corn
Salad
Served with
Fresh Baguettes

Hot Shrimp in
Crispy Wontons
and Celestial
Sauce

Roast Beets and
Roast Vidalia
Onions

Crepes Filled
with Sautéed
Apples, Bananas,
and Rum

SERVES 4–6

This is an excellent summertime menu, which you can serve to your most beloved person—or several hundred others if you wish.

NOTE: *If you've become a devotee of the "serve a starch first" school of thought, you may want to try the shrimp wontons as a first course.*

TRADE SECRETS FROM A THREE-STAR CHEF

Herbed Corn Salad

Fresh corn, just off the cob, is best for this salad, but off-season, you may substitute high-quality frozen corn. Never, never, never attempt to make it with canned corn. In fact, never make anything with canned corn!

1/4	cup extra-virgin olive oil
2	cloves garlic, minced
	Juice of 1 lemon
1/4	cup dry vermouth
1/4	teaspoon fresh thyme
	Pinch of salt and pepper
3	cups corn kernels from the cob (or thoroughly defrosted frozen corn)
1	green pepper, seeded, deribbed, and minced
1	cup minced scallions, white and green parts
1	ripe tomato, seeded and chopped in fine dice
1/4	cup chopped parsley
	Bunch of fresh basil, shredded
	Whole spinach leaves, washed and dried, stems removed, for garnish

Heat the oil on medium heat. In it, cook the garlic with the lemon juice, vermouth, and thyme. Add the salt and pepper. Cook for 5 minutes. Add the corn and simmer 5–7 minutes longer. In a bowl, combine the corn with the peppers, scallions, tomato, parsley, and basil.

Serve at room temperature on a bed of fresh, uncut spinach leaves. Accompany with fresh baguettes.

Do you know the differ-
ence between a TT and a
U-10? If not, you may wind
up buying the wrong size
shrimp for your recipe. Here's
what to know about size:

—TT are known in the
trade as teeny-tiny. They're
river shrimp, and you'll get
anywhere from 500 to
1,000 per pound. TTs are
great for shrimp toast or
shrimp stuffing. Buy a
10-pound frozen "brick"
and use your imagination.

—The next size up is
30–60 per pound. These
are particularly well suited
to casseroles or mayon-
naise-based shrimp salads
used for sandwiches.

—The 16–20s are the per-
fect size for the chef who
requires versatility (they're
used in this shrimp and
wonton recipe). Slightly
smaller, the 21–25s are
good for most purposes.

—Known by the famous
oxymoron "jumbo
shrimp," U-10s and U-12s
(the U stands for "under"
—as in under 10 to a
pound) are showy, but
they're also expensive and
can be tough.

Hot Shrimp in Crispy Wontons and Celestial Sauce

This fundamentally French dish—what could be more French than shrimp, leeks, onions, carrots, basil, and thyme?—is prepared in the Oriental tradition, using wonton skins. Your presentation of it can become an interesting ritual: Try serving the shrimps fanned out on shiny black enamel plates. Artfully arrange the bright green basil leaves either between the shrimp, or in an attractive cluster in the center of the plate.

Try something unexpected: Instead of serving wine with this course, try hot saki served in small sipping cups.

4–6	*raw shrimp per person, #16–20 size, shells removed, and butterflied (see box)*
1	*leek*
1/2	*onion, chopped*
1/2	*rib celery, chopped*
1	*carrot, chopped*
1/4	*teaspoon thyme*
1	*dried bay leaf*
30	*fresh basil leaves*
4	*cups cold water*
1	*tablespoon sweet butter*
1/8	*teaspoon cayenne pepper*
1	*teaspoon salt*
1	*package frozen wonton wrappers, defrosted*
3	*cups vegetable or peanut oil for frying*

Peel the shrimp. In a 2 1/2-quart saucepan, combine the shrimp *shells,* the green part of the leek, the onion, celery, carrot, thyme, bay leaf, 6 of the basil leaves, and the cold water. Boil until the liquid is reduced to 1 1/2 cups. Strain and reserve.

Chop up the white part of the leek and place it in a large sauté pan with 1/4 cup of the reserved stock and the butter; cook over low heat for 3–5 minutes. Remove from the pan and set aside.

Butterfly the shrimp and lay them open on your work surface. Mix the cayenne and salt and sprinkle lightly over all the shrimp. Spread the leek mixture on each opened shrimp. Close up the shrimp.

Place one basil leaf across the center of a wonton wrapper (with one corner facing you), top it with a shrimp, and place another basil leaf on top of the shrimp. Moisten all around the edges of the wonton with water and fold the wrapper over to enclose the shrimp, pressing out the air. Trim with a 3-inch cookie cutter or a sharp knife, into a semicircle. Repeat until all the shrimp are used up.

Heat the oil in a wok or a 2 1/2-quart saucepan until sizzling but not smoking. With a slotted spoon, carefully slide the filled wontons (no more than 4 at a time) into the oil. When the bottoms are golden brown—less than a minute—turn and cook for another 30 seconds. Remove with a slotted spoon and place on paper toweling to drain. Serve immediately, with ramekins of Celestial Sauce (recipe follows).

NOTE: As always, make sure your oil is hot enough (365°) before you attempt to fry the shrimp wontons.

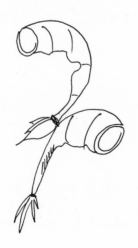

THE WORLD OF WONTONS:

—High-quality, ready-made wontons are available at your local grocer.

—There's nothing to fear when using wonton "skins"—just make sure they're at room temperature, then work quickly to prevent them from drying out.

—Experiment before you tackle this recipe—handle them, fold them, apply water or egg to see how they stick together.

—While you're working on one wonton, keep the rest covered with a damp tea towel. As you finish each wonton, put it on a plate under another damp towel. If you prepare the wontons an hour before frying, cover them with plastic wrap, then with a damp towel, and refrigerate.

—When using wontons to wrap a food such as shrimp, make sure you pat them together carefully but firmly so that you remove all the air. Otherwise, the shrimps will cook unevenly, and the wontons will not be uniform in size.

Celestial Sauce

This delicious sauce is a combination of homemade mayonnaise (it's easy!) and balsamic vinegar. If you love the fruity taste of balsamic, add more if you wish.

1	large egg, at room temperature (see †NOTE, page 83)
	Dash of cayenne
1	teaspoon dry mustard
1	teaspoon salt
1	teaspoon sugar
1 1/4	cups vegetable oil, at room temperature
3	tablespoons fresh lemon juice
3 1/4	tablespoons balsamic vinegar

Put the egg, the dry ingredients, and 1/4 cup of the oil into a blender and mix on high speed for 10 seconds. With the blender running, slowly add another 1/2 cup of oil, then the lemon juice, a tablespoonful at a time, until well blended. Keep the machine running and add the final 1/2 cup of oil, a little at a time, until the mixture is smooth. Add the balsamic vinegar and blend again until smooth. Keep refrigerated until ready to serve.

Roast Beets and Roast Vidalia Onions

You haven't lived until you've tried these—and they couldn't be simpler to prepare. We like to serve them to guests in two courses—a beet followed by an onion (thus, we put the onions in the oven about 10 minutes after the beets, so they're hot when served). If you wish, however, you may serve only one of these delectables during a meal. Always serve them with a knife and a fork. (NOTE: If you insist on serving the beets and onions simultaneously, have a good answer ready when your guests ask where you got the pink onions.)

PREHEAT THE OVEN TO 375°.

For the beets:

4–6	squares of tin foil, 8 × 8 inches
4–6	beets, scrubbed, greens removed
	Salt and pepper
4–6	teaspoons sweet butter

In the center of each piece of foil, place a beet. Wrap completely in foil and twist the ends together securely at the top. Place in a baking dish and bake 45 minutes, or until the beets are fork tender. Remove the foil and, with a sharp knife, carefully remove the skin from the beets. Make an X about 1/4 inch deep in the top of each beet, sprinkle with salt and pepper, and top with a teaspoon of butter. Serve immediately.

For the onions:

4–6	squares of tin foil, 8 × 8 inches
4–6	Vidalia onions, ends trimmed, papery husk removed
4–6	tablespoons extra-virgin olive oil
	Salt and pepper
	Thyme, dried or fresh

(Continued)

Place an onion in the center of each foil square. With a knife, make an X in the top of each onion. Pour 1 tablespoon of oil on top of each onion, sprinkle with salt and pepper, then top with 1/2 teaspoon fresh thyme (1/4 teaspoon if using dried thyme). Fold up the foil and follow the baking instructions given for the beets.

When done, pour the juices that have accumulated at the bottom of the foil over the onions and serve immediately.

Crepes Filled with Sautéed Apples, Bananas, and Rum

To be technical about it, these melt-in-your-mouth French pancakes are really more a dessert than an appetizer. But keep in mind that the crepe is indeed a marvelous foundation for appetizer-type dishes—especially good when the filling is savory.

Make sure you read "Mastering the Art of Crepe-making," below, before you begin.

For the crepes:

1	cup all-purpose flour
3/4	cup cold milk
1/4	cup cold water
3	eggs
	Pinch of salt
5	tablespoons sweet butter, melted

With a whisk, mix the flour, milk, water, eggs, salt, and 2 1/2 tablespoons of the melted butter until thoroughly blended. The consistency should be that of a very thin pancake batter. Refrigerate for at least one hour.

To cook the crepes, using the remaining melted butter to grease your pan, pour 1/4 cup of batter into the center of the pan, and rotate until the batter is distributed evenly. When the bottom is lightly browned—within 20–30 seconds—turn or flip the crepe over and cook it another 15–20 seconds.

(Continued)

For the filling:

2	*sticks (8 ounces) sweet butter*
2–3	*medium-size tart apples (such as Granny Smith), peeled, cored, and cut into 1/2-inch slices*
4	*firm but ripe bananas, peeled, sliced lengthwise, then in half*
1/2	*cup brown sugar*
1/4	*cup rum*

Heat the butter in a large sauté pan until bubbly. Add the apples and cook until they begin to soften. Add the banana sections, sprinkle the brown sugar over all, and stir gently, making sure all the fruit is being glazed. When the bananas are hot to the touch, sprinkle the rum over the entire mixture and gently stir one more time.

Serve immediately, spooning 3–4 banana sections and equal amounts of apple into the center of each crepe. Roll up the crepes and place on individual plates. Drizzle a bit of glaze over the crepes, or serve with sour cream or whipped cream.

TRADE SECRETS FROM A THREE-STAR CHEF

MASTERING THE ART OF CREPE-MAKING

Tip 1—To avoid a rubbery crepe, do not overbeat the batter. If you're whisking by hand, do it quickly; if using an electric mixer, blender, or food processor, pulse on and off until the ingredients are mixed.

Tip 2—Refrigerate your crepe batter for *at least one hour*—three hours is best—before you plan to make the crepes. This allows enough time for the flour to become fully incorporated into the liquid. Lumps will have disappeared, and your batter will have just the right amount of "body" to create a uniform crepe.

Tip 3—Beginners should invest in a nonstick crepe pan (under $10).

Tip 4—To lubricate the pan, use a paper towel shaped into a thick pad; dip the end in melted butter and then quickly smear the butter evenly across the pan. Because it's fast, this method is preferable to using a nonflammable pastry brush. REMINDER: Many a novice has regretted using a cheap, nylon bristle pastry brush for buttering the pan—along with your butter, *it will melt!*

Tip 5—To avoid crepes that are too thick, always use a 1/4 cup measure for pouring the batter—it's the correct amount for a 6-inch crepe.

Tip 6—Pouring the batter can be tricky, so practice a bit until you get the hang of it. With your measuring cup nearly touching the pan, pour the batter quickly into the center, then move the pan back and forth and sideways to distribute it evenly. With a firm flick of the wrist—and a little practice—you'll be able to flip a crepe and catch it in the pan in one elegant motion. (Of course, the old-fashioned way—flipping with a spatula—works fine, too.)

DO-AHEAD MISCELLANY

—Corn salad can be prepared up to two days in advance. Keep it covered and refrigerated. Let stand at room temperature for an hour before serving.

—You may prepare the leek mixture for the shrimps the morning of your party. Keep refrigerated until ready to use.

—The shrimps in wonton can be assembled—but not fried—an hour before you're ready to use them. See box.

—Celestial Sauce can be made in the morning. Cover and refrigerate, but let stand at room temperature for half an hour before serving.

—Beets can be trimmed and onions peeled early in the day. Keep covered at room temperature.

—Crepes can be prepared weeks in advance and frozen; thaw for an hour before using. Or make them in the morning, put them in a large plastic bag, and refrigerate. Let them stand at room temperature for half an hour before serving.

—Apples can be cored and sliced several hours before you need them; sprinkle with lemon juice to prevent discoloring and refrigerate in a plastic bag until ready to use.

NOTE: *Unfilled crepes freeze well, but the rest of the items on this menu do not.*

TRADE SECRETS FROM A THREE-STAR CHEF

12

Oh, Those Little White Lies

GO AHEAD, TELL ONE

When is a sauce not a sauce? Should a skate ray be passed off as a scallop? May a soup be called "fresh" if it isn't? You be the judge:

For the past fifteen years, and once a week on average, Mr. and Mrs. Fezziwig (not their real name) of Southampton have been coming to Anne's restaurants for dinner. Even when she's ensconced in the kitchen and can't see her guests, Anne knows when the Fezziwigs have arrived because, without fail, they always send something back to be recooked, rehashed, or somehow jury-rigged to suit their taste. Upon occasion, she has become exasperated by this ritual, but since they're always thrilled with her transformations—and leave enormous tips for her waiters—she has so far been able to control her natural impulse to put strychnine in their coffee.

But as you must know by now, Anne is not made of stone. Perhaps that's why her self-restraint wavered last spring when Mrs. F. sent back a gorgeous serving of fresh steamed asparagus. Plain, unadorned asparagus, grown locally, picked that morning, and of course, organic.

"It's too crisp," she whispered conspiratorially. "And it hasn't any sauce." Then the unspeakable: "If you have some canned asparagus lying around, I'd really prefer that. And could you put a sauce on it?"

"Fresh" Tomato Soup

Fresh Sea Scallops with Candied Lemon

Mashed Potatoes with Frizzled Leeks

Asparagus au Naturel

Individual Strawberry Shortcakes

SERVES 4–6

In many states—New York, for one—where laws about truth-in-menu are tough, a restaurateur must not only be honest about items listed on the menu, but, when asked by a customer, respond truthfully to questions regarding any food served in the restaurant. The quotes placed around "fresh" tomato soup let customers know it's not. And if there's a query, the secret of the recipe is happily divulged—though as mentioned, few people actually believe it.

STORE-BOUGHT BOUILLON VS. HOMEMADE STOCK

Most of the time, homemade stock is certainly preferable to the cubed or granulated variety. However, the tomato soup recipe requires a hearty liquid to combat the acidity of the tomatoes, and the best and easiest way to get it is by using cubes. NOTE: The bouillon cubes supply the requisite salt, so don't add any of your own.

Anne knew she wouldn't be able to convert this guest to the finer pleasures of fresh vegetables, so she went to work. Destroying the asparagus was easy: She put it back into the steamer for ten minutes until it was limp and its bright, wonderful color was lost to an olive drab. For the final touch, she poured a quarter-cupful of that evening's leek and potato soup over all. Of course, the customer absolutely loved this pabulumy "sauce," and was convinced, thank God, that the asparagus came straight from a can. Who was going to tell her otherwise?

Oh, those little white lies we sometimes have to tell to make people happy. Most of the time, they just sort of happen by accident, don't they? There's never any malice involved—just a desire to keep the peace, to get on with things, to give people what they want. And let's face it, some people just don't want to know the truth—especially when it involves this menu's first course, which Anne takes the liberty of calling "fresh" tomato soup (see box).

As she explains it, "This really is one of the great soups of all time—so good, in fact, that customers have literally begged me for the recipe. Yet when I've hinted that the tomatoes aren't truly fresh—they're truly canned—they refuse to believe it. Everyone is convinced that the only way you can produce this incredibly delicious soup is with handpicked, vine-ripened tomatoes still glistening with morning dew. So what do I do when people ask me how I make it?

"I give them the recipe they *think* they want—which includes lots of fresh tomatoes and hours of prep time for blanching, peeling, seeding, slicing, chopping, and pureeing. Of course, they're always disappointed with the results. Their soup, they say, tastes nothing like mine. Their tomatoes, I reply, probably aren't as good as mine."

And that, dear readers, is the absolute truth.

HOW FRESH—OR HOMEMADE—IS THE FOOD YOU EAT?

Here are some little-known facts about certain foods you may be purchasing at your supermarket and/or eating in restaurants:

Fact: When you buy chicken in an American supermarket, remember that fresh means *not frozen*—and that's all it means. Hence, you can bet that your supermarket chicken was not killed today—or even several months ago. In large markets, packaged birds sit in a "holding tank" hovering around 32 degrees for up to 6 months—and that's what keeps them from going bad.

Fact: Unless you live in Louisiana or Florida, the shrimp you're eating isn't fresh—it's been frozen.

Fact: If you're dining at restaurants that feature entrées in the $12 to $20 range, you can bet those fancy hors d'oeuvres—rumaki or any finger food made with phyllo dough or grape leaves—were not made on the premises. Chances are they arrived, via a manufacturer, in frozen sheets, as did the "specialties" such as stuffed pork chops, stuffed Cornish hens or quail, or even simple desserts. All are available—frozen—from professional food purveyors across the country.

Fact: When you order French fries—the great "American" food that is the single biggest money-maker in the restaurant business—do you picture someone in the kitchen peeling potatoes and then putting them through a mandoline? Forget it. Unless they're served in the most upscale of restaurants, you're getting once-frozen, precut, machine-cut fries. Likewise, the "beer-battered" shrimp you order. Nobody's in the kitchen hand-dipping shrimp into batter. Those tasty morsels travel from their frozen shipping carton to the deep fryer in a flick of the wrist.

Fact: The customer has the right to ask about the origin of a dish, and the restaurant is obligated to tell the truth.

Fact: You may not like what you hear.

"Fresh" Tomato Soup

We're happy to report that a Long Island restaurant critic said this soup had "the taste and texture of August beefsteaks."

1	tablespoon extra-virgin olive oil
1	bunch scallions, white and green parts, finely chopped
One	28-ounce can crushed tomatoes*
One	28-ounce can cold water
1	large cube (or 2 small cubes) Knorr Chicken bouillon†
2	tablespoons sugar
1/4	teaspoon each of the following dried ground herbs: rosemary, thyme, marjoram, oregano, bay leaf, and basil

Pour the oil into a 3 1/2-quart pot, heat until sizzling, and add the minced scallions. Sauté until limp but not brown. Add the tomatoes, water, bouillon cube(s), sugar, and ground herbs and mix well. Heat until the soup comes to a simmer, stirring occasionally. Serve hot.

*Make sure the can specifies "crushed" tomatoes. Do not use pureed tomatoes, whole tomatoes, stewed tomatoes, or any canned tomato product that also contains basil, bay leaves, or other herbs and spices.

†Do not substitute homemade chicken stock for the bouillon cube(s) and water. See box.

Fresh Sea Scallops with Candied Lemon

If you like the taste of lemon with seafood, you'll love this dish. It's also a snap to make—ready to serve in just 4–5 minutes.

2	lemons, quartered, seeds removed
1/2	cup sugar, in a bowl
8	ounces (2 sticks) sweet butter
2	pounds medium sea scallops (or 1/3 pound per person)
	Pepper
Optional:	3 sprigs cilantro, for garnish

Toss the lemon quarters in the sugar until lightly coated, then remove from the bowl and set aside. Melt the butter in a 14-inch sauté pan and heat until bubbly. Add the sugar-coated lemon quarters and toss; add the scallops and a touch of pepper and sauté, gently tossing all the ingredients until the scallops turn a lovely brown color and are barely firm to the touch.

Remove the scallops and lemons to a platter; garnish with a few sprigs of cilantro if you wish, and serve immediately.

BUYER BEWARE: When purchasing scallops, make sure you're getting the real thing. Many a neophyte has been duped into buying skate ray, a cartilaginous fish that can be stamped into little rounds that look like scallops! Ask your fishperson, who is obliged, by law, to tell you the truth.

—The best potatoes for mashing are Idaho or russet—they have a wonderful nutty flavor and are also inexpensive. Yukon golds are terrific mashed, but too expensive to use in this chapter's recipe. Never mash red bliss or California white-skinned— they're best boiled or steamed.

—The so-called "chef's potato"—also known as the green mountain, katonah, or "all-purpose" potato—should never be used for any purpose. They're big, ugly, and unwieldly, but most important, they're waterlogged. (That's why they're most often used in steamtable operations—they don't dry out for hours and hours.)

—While peeling a potato, should you notice a layer of green beneath the peel, do not use it—it's solanine, a poisonous alkaloid. Return the suspect spud (and the entire bag it came from) to your green grocer.

Mashed Potatoes with Frizzled Leeks

True or False: If you puree potatoes, you should call them mashed. We don't think so (but then, we'd never serve pureed potatoes by any name—except maybe "baby food").

Incredibly rich, these are the real thing, which means they should have a few lumps.

6–8	*Idaho or russet potatoes, peeled and quartered (see box)*
2	*eggs, well beaten (optional) (see †NOTE, page 83)*
1	*ounce (2 tablespoons) sweet butter, melted*
	Salt and pepper to taste
1/2	*cup heavy cream*

Place the potatoes in a 3 1/2-quart pot and add cold water to cover. Boil for 20–25 minutes or until tender. Drain completely. Put the potatoes through a ricer or mash them well, then add the eggs, butter, and seasonings. Mash again. Add the heavy cream and whip all ingredients with a wooden spoon. Serve immediately or place in the refrigerator until ready to serve, then reheat in a 350° oven for 20 minutes.

VARIATION: If you prepare them early in the day, the potatoes will form a natural crust, which will add another texture to the meal.

Frizzled Leeks

Sometimes known as "frizzed" leeks, these have a subtle flavor, a crisp texture, and a beautiful brown color. They're wonderful sprinkled on mashed potatoes, or used as a sophisticated garnish for many other dishes. Very professional-looking!

6   medium leeks, washed, root ends and green stems
      removed

3   cups vegetable oil

Insert the fine slicing ("F") disk into your Cuisinart. Remove the large pusher assembly and place one leek in a horizontal position (on its side) onto the disc. Return the pusher to its original position, press down, and pulse.* Repeat until all the leeks have been sliced. Rinse them under cold water, spread on paper towels, and pat dry.

In a wok or other deep pan used for frying, pour the oil and heat to 365°. (A leek strip should sizzle briskly and immediately when you place it in the oil.)

With a slotted spoon, carefully put in one batch of leeks at a time; move them around in the oil to separate any pieces that might be sticking together. When the leeks are nicely browned, remove them with a slotted spoon and place on paper towels to drain. (Continue until all are done.) Set aside, uncovered and unrefrigerated, until ready to serve.

WHEN FRYING FRIZZLED LEEKS...

...remember that the temperature of the oil is the key to success! When the oil hovers around 365°, the leeks fry quickly and evenly and turn a lovely brown. A lower temperature results in greasy, greenish-brown leeks; a higher temperature, burnt and blackened ones. When a chopstick (or wooden spoon) inserted into oil begins to sizzle, the temperature is right.

Asparagus au Naturel

*Asparagus is so delicious, we like to serve it lightly steamed
and plain. Au naturel is best, too, with this particular menu,
where you don't want a sauce competing with the candied lemon
sauce of the scallops.*

6–8   asparagus spears per person, about 1 inch trimmed
       from the bottoms

At the bottom of a large pot, position your steamer (see box)
and pour in one inch of cold water. Stand the asparagus on their
ends and lean the spears against the sides of the pot so that
they're standing upright. Cover the pot. Bring the water to a boil
and let the spears steam 4–5 minutes, until they're hot to the
touch but crispy. Serve immediately (or see "Do-Ahead
Miscellany").

HOW TO AVOID OVERCOOKED ASPARAGUS

Remember to remove the cover of your pot when the vegetables are done or they will continue to cook until they turn
to mush. If you're not serving at once, it's best to remove the
asparagus from the pot and immediately plunge them into
cold water to stop the cooking. A quick steaming just before
serving will reheat them.

Individual Strawberry Shortcakes

You will be surprised at the number of guests who haven't had real strawberry shortcake for years. At dinner parties, one can let friends assemble their own, which they will love. Be forewarned: You'll need plenty of extra strawberries and whipped cream on hand.

PREHEAT THE OVEN TO 450°.

2	cups flour
3	tablespoons sugar
2	teaspoons baking powder
1/4	teaspoon baking soda
1/2	teaspoon salt
1/4	cup plus 1 tablespoon sweet butter, chilled
2/3	cup buttermilk
2–3	quarts fresh strawberries, washed, dried, and hulled
1/2	teaspoon vanilla extract or bourbon
2–3	tablespoons sifted confectioner's sugar
1	cup cold heavy cream

YIELD: ABOUT 3 CUPS WHIPPED CREAM

To make the shortcake pastry, put the dry ingredients in a large bowl and mix well. Add the butter and quickly mix with your fingertips or with a pastry blender until mixture looks like small particles of grain. Add the buttermilk and, with a fork, mix until a soft dough forms.

On a lightly floured surface, gently knead the dough about 10 times. Pat it out to a thickness of 3/4 inch, and cut into 2 1/2-inch rounds with a cookie cutter or an inverted drinking glass.

(Continued)

OH, THOSE LITTLE WHITE LIES

Place the rounds 2 inches apart on an ungreased cookie sheet and bake for 12–15 minutes, until a medium golden brown. When done, place the shortcakes on a rack to cool, and cover them with a tea towel to keep in the moisture.

Prepare the strawberries and set aside.

Add the vanilla or bourbon and the confectioner's sugar to the cream and whip with a hand mixer for 3–5 minutes.

To serve, place the shortcakes on a large platter, and put the strawberries and whipped cream in separate serving bowls with spoons. Do this buffet style at one end of the table, so your guests can line up to assemble their own desserts and then seat themselves at the table.

DO-AHEAD MISCELLANY

—You may prepare the tomato soup up to a week ahead of time. Keep it covered, in the refrigerator, but make sure you remove it the morning of your dinner party so that it is at room temperature when you begin to reheat it.

—As mentioned, if you prepare your mashed potatoes in the morning, they'll form an interesting crust, which will add texture to the meal.

—Frizzled leeks can be prepared up to 2 hours prior to serving, as long as you keep them uncovered in a very dry place. Don't heap them into a pile—rather, spread them out on a dish towel or paper towel.

—If you cannot bear to prepare the asparagus at the last minute (which is the *best* time to do it), you may precook them early in the day, but make sure you cook them only halfway through.

—The shortcakes may be made early in the day. Cover them with a tea towel until they're cooled; then place them in a plastic bag with the end left open.

NOTE: *The shortcakes freeze well if you follow the cooling instructions above, then wrap them securely in plastic wrap. The rest of the items on this menu do not freeze well.*

TRADE SECRETS FROM A THREE-STAR CHEF

13

The Buffet Supper with a Hidden Agenda

HOST A "PAY THEM ALL BACK" PARTY

$\mathcal{S}$hould you give a party because you feel obligated to do so? Sure, but only on one condition: In the process, you must be able to cross off your list most of those social "paybacks" that have been nagging at your conscience all year—that friendly couple you met at Cancun who turned out to live only thirty minutes away; that dreary woman you met at Smokers' Anonymous who keeps wanting the two of you to "do" lunch; the neighbors who belong to the same country club but who never remember your name; the young couple who just moved to town whom your boss's wife asked you to "introduce around." Imagine! With a little advanced planning and a super (but easy) buffet menu, you can invite them all at once and wipe the slate clean.

The trick here is to invite six or eight of your *real* friends to mix in and provide the social lubrication to keep the conversation flowing. Wait for warm weather so people can circulate in and out of doors and not get stuck in a corner with a stranger. Then, devise a culinary battle plan that keeps the evening, and the edibles, moving right along. With the right mix of food and people, it won't even matter if someone asks at the last minute to bring extra guests—like their two punked-out teenage kids with neon hair who are wired to their Walkmen and speak only in hip-hop.

*Mussels
Mandarin*

*Roast Pork Loin
with Rosemary*

Tomato Aspic

*Orange Almond
Salad*

*Orzo and Pepper
Casserole*

*Cranberry-
Walnut Cake*

SERVES 12–16

Here, then, are copious tips and hints gleaned from our experiences entertaining friends and neighbors, and from Anne's years as chef at the Hedges House restaurant in East Hampton. At that tony location, her buffet brunch drew a crowd of regulars, including one reviewer who said he couldn't "imagine a more felicitous place to spend a few hours on Sunday afternoon."

—*You won't need as much food as you'd think:* In the restaurant business, a buffet translates to "all you can eat," and indeed, when people are *paying,* they'll storm the table, eat until it comes out of their ears, and try to steal your spoons besides. The buffet-at-home, however, is a far less predatory affair. Rule of thumb: Most people eat *half* (or less) of what you'd consider a normal-size serving, and if there's enough variety—six dishes is a perfect number—the portion sizes become even smaller.

—*Serve at least one "unusual" item:* We're not talking eel salad or sweetbreads on toast here. Just give your guests something unpredictable, interesting, hot or spicy, a dish they've maybe never had before. Rein yourself in at two novel items, though. If they're a hit and you run out, or if they bomb and just sit there, you've still got four more items to work with.

—*Avoid a six-course "chew-a-thon":* Think through your menu and ask yourself, How much effort is involved in eating all this food? Then strive for a balance so guests don't give up, get tired, or choke to death. The "payback" menu has a 2 to 6 ratio of chewy to nonchewy foods: the mussels and pork require fairly serious mastication, while the rest could be gummed or swallowed whole, depending on guests' dental condition and knowledge of etiquette.

—*Practice the "bait & switch" technique:* During "intermissions," when people are busy chatting or trying to pocket your silver, rotate the serving dishes, then introduce a "new" item—a large bowl of salad, for example. When guests turn their attention back to the table, they'll be surprised and delighted to see yet another offering.

TRADE SECRETS FROM A THREE-STAR CHEF

—*Keep serving dishes attractive at all times:* Even if your guests *do* behave like horses feeding at a trough, your table doesn't have to show it. After the salad has been attacked, refill the bowl or at least "fluff" the greens so they still look attractive. Likewise, tidy up slices of meat or pieces of cake or bread. Remove crumbs and olive pits, and clean up spills along the way. Depending on the crowd, you may need to rake your carpet to get at ground-in radishes. Consider hiring a helper for such chores.

—*Remember the secret of "filler food":* You want people to leave feeling satisfied—and you want to make sure they leave, period—so make sure you've got filler food: plenty of bread—the cranberry cake plus some baguettes would be perfect—and at least one other high-starch item, such as the orzo casserole. Side benefit: Fillers are usually the most inexpensive items on the menu.

—*MOST IMPORTANT RULE: Never serve shrimp at a buffet.* Here's where the "you won't need as much food as you'd think" theory falls apart. Want to know the sound of a cyclone? Always wished you could visit a hog farm? Just bring on these tasty little crustaceans. Then get out of the way!

With all that in mind, let's move to the menu.

Mussels Mandarin

Anne's recipe for the Mandarin sauce has appeared in Gourmet *magazine—a request from a reader in the "You Asked For It" column.*

2	cups water
	Bouquet garni (see box)
1	dozen mussels per person, scrubbed and debearded (see box)

For the sauce:

2	cups Kikkoman soy sauce
2	cups sesame oil
1/2	cup apple cider vinegar
1 1/2	cups sugar
1	bunch scallions, chopped in 2-inch pieces (including green part), for garnish

In a large stock pot, bring the water to a boil over high heat. Add the bouquet garni and the mussels and bring the water back to the boil. Cover the pot and cook the mussels until they open, about 6–8 minutes. Remove the mussels from the pot, drain, and place them in a large casserole dish. Leave the mussels in their shells. (Discard the liquid and bouquet garni and any unopened mussels.)

Whisk together the soy sauce and all remaining sauce ingredients until well blended. Pour over the mussels and allow them to marinate in the refrigerator for at least 3 hours.

Just before serving, pour off most of the sauce and save it for other uses.

Place the mussels on a large platter and sprinkle with the scallions. Serve immediately.

Roast Pork Loin with Rosemary

Slow cooking is the secret to this succulent roast pork loin.

PREHEAT THE OVEN TO 325°.

One	*4-pound boneless loin of pork*
2	*large cloves garlic, thinly sliced*
2	*teaspoons dried rosemary*
	Pepper
4	*tablespoons Kikkoman soy sauce*
1/2	*cup dry vermouth*
	Sprigs of fresh rosemary, for garnish

Place the pork loin, fatty side up, on a work surface. With a sharp knife, make several slits in the meat about 1/4 inch deep. Into the slits insert slivers of garlic, bits of rosemary, and a little pepper.

Put the pork loin in a 10 × 12 roasting pan. Pour the soy sauce over the loin, then the vermouth. Add just enough water to come 1/4 of the way up the pork loin.

Bake in the oven for about 1 1/2 hours, or until a thermometer registers 155°. *Do not overcook*—the pork will be light pink in the center. See box.

Remove the roast from the oven and let it rest for at least 5 minutes. Then slice it in 1/4-inch slices and arrange them on a platter. Use sprigs of fresh rosemary for garnish.

PORK PRIMER

Remember the way your mother roasted pork—for days, until it turned gray? Times have changed! It's quite safe, says the National Pork Producers' Council—and we know it's much tastier—to serve pork that's slightly pink, as long as the internal temperature is around 160°. To achieve this temperature in a pork loin roast, remove it from the oven when an instant thermometer reads 155°, then let the roast sit for 5 minutes until the temperature hits 160°.

Tomato Aspic

Shimmery and colorful, this aspic adds zip to any buffet table.

2 1/2	envelopes Knox unflavored gelatin
3 1/2	cups thick *tomato juice* (preferably Sacramento)
4	tablespoons sweet butter
3	large ribs celery, with leaves, finely chopped
1	clove garlic, finely chopped
2	medium onions, finely chopped
6	medium-size tomatoes, quartered
	Juice and grated rind of one lemon
1 1/2	tablespoons Worcestershire sauce
2	dried bay leaves
3	whole cloves
1	teaspoon dried tarragon
2	teaspoons sugar
1	teaspoon salt
8	peppercorns

Grease a 2-quart ring mold or Bundt-type pan.

In a large mixing bowl, sprinkle the gelatin over 1 cup of the tomato juice and allow it to soften for about 10 minutes. Stir occasionally, then set aside.

In a soup kettle or stock pot, heat the butter on medium heat and cook the celery, garlic, and onions for 10 minutes. Add the tomatoes, the remaining 2 1/2 cups of tomato juice, the lemon juice and rind, Worcestershire, bay leaves, cloves, tarragon, sugar, salt, and peppercorns. Bring to a boil, then immediately reduce the heat to low and simmer, uncovered, for 45 minutes.

Strain the cooked tomato mixture through a mesh strainer,

forcing through as much vegetable pulp as possible. Discard the residue.

Add the strained tomato mixture to the gelatin mixture and stir until completely blended.

Pour into the prepared mold and chill for at least 6 hours.

To serve, unmold the aspic onto a serving platter. (If you wish, you may line the platter with your choice of lettuce leaves.)

Orange Almond Salad

Valencia oranges are fine in this salad, but if you can get "blood oranges" at your greengrocer, so much the better.

4	tablespoons apple cider vinegar
1/2	cup vegetable oil
2	tablespoons honey
1/2	teaspoon Dijon mustard
1 1/2	tablespoons butter
1	cup slivered almonds, toasted
3 to 4	large heads romaine, washed, dried, and torn into bite-size pieces
2 to 3	ripe oranges, peeled, seeded, sliced into 1/4-inch wedges

Whisk together the first four ingredients and set aside.

Melt the butter in a medium sauté pan over medium heat. When bubbly, add the almonds and sauté until they just begin to brown. Remove them from the pan and place them on paper toweling to drain.

In a large salad bowl, place the lettuce pieces and orange wedges. Add the honey-mustard dressing and toss with your hands until the lettuce is lightly coated. Just before serving, toss the almonds into the salad.

Serve immediately.

Orzo and Pepper Casserole

If you're feeling adventurous, add some of your favorite vegetables to this dish. Chopped zucchini works well; so do tender green peas.

PREHEAT THE OVEN TO 325°.

4	tablespoons olive oil
1	red onion, finely chopped
2	jalapeño peppers, finely chopped
3	tomatoes, peeled and coarsely chopped
2	tablespoons sugar
One	16-ounce package Orzo, cooked according to package directions; substitute low-sodium chicken stock for water
	Salt and pepper to taste
1	cup finely grated white Cheddar cheese

Heat the olive oil in a large sauté pan on medium flame until bubbling but not smoking. Add the onion and peppers and sauté for 5 minutes, or until the onion is translucent. Add tomatoes and sugar and continue to cook on medium for another 5 minutes. Remove from the heat.

Put the orzo and the tomato mixture into a 2 1/2-quart casserole dish and mix until all ingredients are blended. Taste and adjust the seasoning with salt and pepper. Sprinkle the grated cheese over the top.

Bake for 20 minutes, or until the cheese bubbles and turns golden brown.

Serve hot or at room temperature.

Cranberry-Walnut Cake

This wonderful "cake" has a breadlike texture. It goes beautifully with the pork roast and the rest of the buffet offerings, yet it's sweet enough for those who still have room for dessert.

PREHEAT THE OVEN TO 350°.

1	cup frozen cranberries
3	cups all-purpose flour
1/2	cup plus 2 tablespoons sugar or vanilla sugar (see page 157)
1	teaspoon baking soda
1	tablespoon baking powder
1 1/2	teaspoons kosher salt
1/2	cup walnuts, coarsely chopped
1	teaspoon orange or lemon zest
1	cup buttermilk
3/4	cup plain yogurt
2	tablespoons sweet butter, melted
2	large eggs, beaten

Generously grease a 10-inch springform pan with butter or margarine. Line the bottom of the pan with waxed paper and grease the paper. Set aside.

Chop the cranberries by placing them, unthawed, in a Cuisinart fitted with the steel blade. Pulse at least 10 times until coarsely chopped.

In a large bowl, mix together all the dry ingredients. Add the cranberries, nuts, and zest to the dry mixture and mix until well dusted.

In a 2-cup measuring cup or a small bowl, whisk together the buttermilk, yogurt, melted butter, and beaten eggs.

Pour the liquid into the dry ingredients and mix until just blended. Do not overmix.

Spoon the mixture evenly into the springform pan. If necessary, gently pat the top of the batter with a spatula to even it.

Bake in the preheated oven for 50–55 minutes. The top should be golden brown and a toothpick inserted in the center should come out clean.

Cool for 10 minutes while still in the pan. Then remove the springform and allow the cake to rest another 5 minutes. Remove the bottom of the pan and gently pull the waxed paper from the cake.

Serve warm or at room temperature.

DO-AHEAD MISCELLANY

—Make your mussel marinade days or weeks in advance if you wish. You may clean the mussels in the morning, but keep them refrigerated until ready to steam.

—The pork loin may be roasted a day ahead of time; keep it covered in the refrigerator, but bring it to room temperature before serving.

—The tomato aspic can be made the night before. Keep refrigerated but do not cover.

—The salad greens can be torn, washed, and dried hours before serving. Keep them loosely covered in the refrigerator. The salad dressing can be prepared days ahead. Keep the sectioned oranges in a plastic bag in the refrigerator.

—The orzo casserole can be assembled (except for the cheese) up to 2 days ahead. Keep it covered in the refrigerator.

—The cranberry-walnut cake can be made one day in advance. Be sure it cools completely, then store it in a sealed plastic bag. Do not refrigerate.

NOTE: *The items on this menu do not freeze well.*

14

It's Time to Get Over Those Food Phobias

A MENU TO MAKE CONVERTS OF THEM ALL

"Eat your prunes," the Scottish mother told her son.

"I dinna want my prunes," he replied.

"You must eat your prunes or you wilna get your porridge."

"I wilna eat my prunes."

"God will be very angry if ye dinna eat your prunes."

"Let him be angry then, I wilna eat my prunes."

So the mother grabbed the lad by his ear and marched him upstairs to his bedroom, telling him "Ye will stay in your room till you decide to eat your prunes."

About an hour later, a terrible storm began to blow about the cottage, with sheets of rain and crashing thunder and great bolts of lightning. Fearing her son would be frightened, the mother went upstairs and quietly opened the door, expecting to find the boy cowering under the covers. Instead she found him staring out the window, his chin in his hands, his elbows on the sill, gently shaking his head.

"Tsk, tsk, tsk," he was repeating softly. "Sich a fuss over six prunes."

This little story illustrates an important point: that parents can powerfully influence children's attitudes and beliefs about food. How do they do it? The Guilt-Trip-from-God is one effec-

---

Garlic-Steamed Little Neck Clams

Sautéed Soft-Shell Crabs

Curried Carrot Salad

Hot Buttered Corn Bread

Crème Brûlée

SERVES 4–6

---

tive way. Then there's the turned-up nose, the pursed lips, the whole-body shudder when they come in contact with a food they dislike.

Sometimes, however, the real culprit is improperly prepared food: spinach cooked beyond recognition, meat cooked for so long it resembles—and tastes like—shoe leather. All these contribute to kids' food phobias. And more often than not, the phobias stay with them into adulthood, when they pass their fears on to their own children. What a pity!

We're sure you can think of examples from your own childhood. Perhaps they're similar to our own—and those of friends and acquaintances we talked to while doing this chapter. Here are just a few examples:

—"Why I Hate Okra," by Anne Matthews. I hate okra because when I was growing up, my grandmother, a Southern woman of immense regional American cooking talent, decided one day she was going to make a shrimp gumbo. Into the kitchen came all these wonderful ingredients, including fresh okra. I had never seen it before and I said, "Amma, what is that?" and she said, "It's okra, honey. You gotta have it in a gumbo, otherwise it's not a gumbo." After the gumbo had been cooking for a while, she wanted me to sample the okra, so she pulled a piece of it out of the pot and handed it to me and said, "Here, have a bite." There, dangling before me, was this slimy long gelatinous-looking thing, dripping out of the pot. I've not been able to eat okra since—a shame really, since I'm told it's actually quite good (as long as you don't eat too much of it).

—Why would anyone dislike *any* part of French bread? Ask our friend, a genuine Boston Brahmin, who attended Groton and Harvard and went on to become a heavy hitter in the publishing world. As he explains it, "Mummy believed that the soft, inner part of French bread was fattening and would interfere with proper digestion. Whenever bread was served, she pulled it apart and ate only the crust, preferably the heel of the loaf. Of course, my siblings and I followed her lead. To this day, each of us *must* remove the insides of any type of soft bread. It's a compulsion. We just pile it up alongside our plates and hope the servants will come along and dispose of it."

TRADE SECRETS FROM A THREE-STAR CHEF

—When people tell you they can't stand eating organ meats such as liver, nine times out of ten their revulsion originated with a parent. Nancy concurs: "Although my father did most of the cooking for our family, it was my mother who often came up with the ideas for what we'd have for dinner. One of her favorite meals—a real craving of hers—was calve's liver smothered in fried onions. I never really liked the smell of this dish and complained bitterly about it, but to tell you the truth, I was almost willing to try it—until that fateful day when I asked her why she liked eating something I found so peculiar. As soon as she said, 'It's not strange; you have a liver, and a little baby calf has a liver, too,' I knew this was a food that would never touch my lips. Never has—and never will!"

—We know of a former college professor who has a particular aversion to lobster—even though this chap is a *native* of eastern Long Island, an area famous for its wonderful, fresh-caught shellfish. How could something so ridiculous happen? He's confided in us—on promise of anonymity—that he shuns lobster because every time his father plunged a live one into a pot of boiling water, he'd shout, "I just hope this one isn't God!"

We hope the message is loud and clear: Whether you're a parent or not, if you love food, you *must* take seriously your role as an educator of young palates. And to help you do it, we've developed a menu that's full of things certain adult people think they don't like—until they try them.

For example, guests who think clams taste like mushy rubber bands will snap to attention when they taste our delicious garlic-steamed clams. And our soft-shell crab recipe—complete with instructions for hypnotizing the little critters—will convert even the most squeamish of God-fearing friends, no matter what their age. When you think of corn bread, does the Colonel come to mind? Not after tonight. Know of someone who hates curry? Try our Curried Carrot Salad—then be prepared to hand out the recipe.

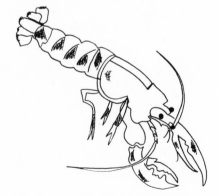

The final touch is a safe bet: Crème Brûlée, which no one on the planet doesn't like, and almost no one knows how to make properly.

IT'S TIME TO GET OVER THOSE FOOD PHOBIAS

Flaming removes the alcohol taste. Quickly touch the edge of your pan with the flame from a match; the liquid will ignite and the flames will die in less than 30 seconds. (Practiced chefs simply tilt the pan toward the flame from the stove, then quickly and carefully right the pan while waiting until the flames die.)

Reducing evaporates and condenses sauces so their flavor is intensified. The liquid must not be boiled; it should be "cooked" at a simmer to truly meld the flavors. The process takes time—anywhere from 12 to 20 minutes or more, depending on the amount of liquid to be reduced.

NOTE: *Sauces containing eggs cannot be reduced; long-term heat will only scramble the eggs.*

Garlic-Steamed Little Neck Clams

This recipe produces a chowderlike first course. Serve it with chewy baguettes, so your guests can sop up all the juices.

1	tablespoon minced garlic
2	cups chopped onions
3	cups chopped red bell pepper
1/3	cup olive oil
1 1/2	cups dry vermouth
6	cups chicken stock
	Dried red pepper flakes, to taste
2	cups ripe tomatoes, peeled, seeded, and chopped (or canned plum tomatoes, drained and chopped)
60–72	little neck clams, well scrubbed (see box, page 151)
	Chopped fresh parsley, for garnish

In a 12-inch skillet, sauté the garlic and onions and the red pepper in the olive oil on a low flame for about 8 minutes. Turn up the heat to medium-high, add the vermouth and flame (see box) for about 30 seconds. Stir in the chicken stock and cook on medium flame, until the liquid is reduced to approximately 4 1/2 cups. Add red pepper flakes to taste and the chopped tomatoes. Mix well.

Fifteen minutes before serving time, heat the broth to boiling, add the clams, cover, and cook until the clams open, about 5–7 minutes.

To serve, ladle broth and clams into serving bowls and garnish with chopped parsley. Serve with cocktail forks and soup spoons.

VARIATION: *As an appetizer for a lighter meal, the broth and clam mixture can also be poured over small portions of linguine or spaghetti.*

ALL ABOUT CLAMS

If you're at all nervous about eating clams or buying them, ask your purveyor to show you the document (usually a sticker) that certifies their origin, size, and type, and that guarantees they came from water that tested clean and free of pollutants. Clams cannot be sold legally without this sticker, so if it cannot be produced for your perusal, shop elsewhere.

When ordering clams, ask your fish person to select "matched" necks, so you get clams that are all the same size—important when serving cooked clams. (If, on another occasion, you serve raw clams, "mixed" necks—of different sizes—are fine.)

To clean, place the clams in a large bowl with enough cold water to cover, and add 1/4 cup salt. Let them sit for several hours, then rinse thoroughly. If the water is still sandy, rinse again.

NOTE: *If a clam opens before you cook it, throw it out, it's already dead. If it doesn't open during steaming, toss it—it's not meant to be eaten.*

Soft-shell crabs can be dangerous during the cooking process, because their juices can cause hot oil to sputter and spit. Therefore, (1) dry them as much as possible before cooking; (2) squeeze them gently with a spatula before placing them in oil; and (3) never cook them when you're scantily clad. Long oven mitts are a must!

WHICH SIZE CRAB?

Three choices are usually available: hotel (the smallest, serve 4–6 per person); prime (medium, serve 3 per person); and jumbo (serve 2). Preparation is the same for all sizes, but you must reduce the cooking time accordingly.

HOW TO HYPNOTIZE A CRAB

If you can't bear to kill a crab because you think it knows what you're doing, try hypnotizing the little critter first. Turn the crab on its back, then stroke its tummy with your finger. Within seconds, the crab will be under your spell. Coward's alternative: Buy your crabs "ready for cooking."

Sautéed Soft-Shell Crabs

Although you may use vegetable oil in your sauté pan, we think sweet butter is the perfect cooking medium to enhance the taste of these sweet morsels. (Do not use olive oil or peanut oil, both of which impart an inappropriate flavor.)

8–12	*large soft-shell crabs (see box)*
1	*cup flour*
1	*tablespoon pepper*
1	*teaspoon salt*
1	*teaspoon cayenne pepper*
8	*tablespoons (1 stick) sweet butter*
	Lemon wedges (2 per person)
	Parsley sprigs, for garnish

Wash and thoroughly dry the prepared crabs; set them aside on paper toweling. Mix the flour, pepper, salt, and cayenne and distribute it evenly on a large platter. Dredge each crab in the flour, shake off the excess, and set aside.

Melt the butter in a 12-inch sauté pan over medium flame and heat until the butter is bubbly but not smoking. Sauté four crabs at a time, cooking them 1 1/2 minutes per side, or until each side turns reddish-brown. Remove from the pan and place it on a rack in a 300° oven to keep it warm while you cook the remaining crabs.

To serve, arrange the crabs on a large platter or on individual plates and garnish with wedges of lemon and sprigs of parsley.

Curried Carrot Salad

This is a colorful and fun salad to make. With your trusty Cuisinart, you can create almost any texture you like—from fine grate to lightly shredded or coarsely chopped—and do so in a matter of minutes.

6	carrots, peeled, ends removed
2	garlic cloves, finely minced
1/4	cup white wine vinegar
3	tablespoons extra-virgin olive oil
1	tablespoon curry powder
	Salt and pepper to taste

With your Cuisinart, process the carrots with (1) the fine or medium shredding disk, (2) the fine julienne disk, or (3) the metal blade. Pulse until the carrots are grated to the texture you want. Put the carrots in a large bowl and add the garlic, vinegar, oil, and curry. (If you're new to curry, you may want to add it in small increments and taste before adding more.) Mix all ingredients thoroughly. Let rest for 15 minutes so that the flavors are absorbed by the carrots (do not refrigerate). Just before serving, taste the mixture, and if desired, add salt and pepper to taste. Serve over romaine lettuce leaves on individual salad plates.

NOTE: *Ever wrestled with a romaine leaf to get it to lie flat on the plate? Turn it "face" down, then firmly pound the center until the spiny part breaks. You may have to do this in two places along the spine.*

Hot Buttered Corn Bread

You can make this from scratch if you have time, but why bother? There are several excellent *brands—Jiffy, Dromedary, George Washington—that produce high-quality corn bread, and all you have to do is add one "secret" ingredient to make it taste homemade. Here's how:*

Follow the directions on the package of corn bread mix. Use 2 boxes for 12 muffins or an 8-inch-square baking pan. Secret ingredient: Add 2 tablespoons bacon drippings. *Do not overmix.* Spoon the mixture into the prepared pan or muffin cups and bake according to instructions on the box. Serve piping hot, with lots of sweet butter.

Or if you have the time and the inclination, here's a terrific "scratch" recipe:

PREHEAT THE OVEN TO 425°.

1	cup yellow cornmeal
1	cup all-purpose flour
1/4	cup sugar
3	teaspoons baking powder
1/4	teaspoon baking soda
1	teaspoon salt
1	cup fresh corn (or frozen corn, defrosted and rinsed)
2	eggs
1	cup buttermilk
2	tablespoons melted sweet butter, vegetable oil, or bacon drippings
Optional:	1/2 teaspoon red pepper flakes

Grease an 8-inch square baking pan or a 12-cup muffin tin. Mix all the dry ingredients including the corn (and if you wish, the red pepper flakes) together in a large bowl. In a smaller bowl, beat the eggs and blend in the buttermilk and oil. Add the liquids to the dry ingredients and mix quickly with a fork. *Do not overmix.* Scoop the mixture into the pan or muffin tin (2/3 full for muffins) and bake for 25 minutes. Remove from the oven and allow the corn bread to rest for 10 minutes before serving.

Crème Brûlée

How can a dish called "burnt cream" be so delicious? Three reasons: a rich vanilla flavor, contrasting textures (soft vs. hard), and contrasting temperatures (cold vs. hot).

PREHEAT THE OVEN TO 300°.

3	cups heavy cream
6	tablespoons sugar or vanilla sugar (see page 157)
6	egg yolks
2	teaspoons vanilla extract (no imitations, please!)
1/2	cup light brown granulated or "brownulated" sugar

For lots of "no-fail" trade secrets about crème brûlée, please read the box before proceeding.

In a 1 1/2-quart saucepan, heat the cream to just below a simmer and stir in the sugar. Do not boil. In a large bowl, beat the egg yolks until light in color and add the hot cream slowly, stirring all the while. Add the vanilla. Using cheesecloth or a sieve, strain the liquid into individual 6-ounce ramekins.

Set the ramekins in a large pan filled with 1 inch of very hot water. Place in the oven and bake for 50 minutes, or until a tester comes out clean. Allow to cool, then place the ramekins in the refrigerator for at least 4 hours. *Do not cover with foil or plastic wrap.*

Before serving, preheat the broiler. Place the ramekins on a cookie sheet, then sprinkle the top of each creme with enough brown sugar to cover, roughly a scant tablespoonful. Place the ramekins under the broiler (about 4–5 inches from the heat) for about 5–7 seconds, until the sugar caramelizes and starts to bubble. Serve immediately.

VANILLA SUGAR

Pour 1 pound grandulated white or turbinado sugar or 1/2 pound superfine sugar into a glass jar. Slice one vanilla bean lengthwise (use a razor or scissors), flatten it as best you can, then cut it into half-inch pieces. Bury the vanilla in the sugar and allow it to age for one month, mixing occasionally. This adds depth to any recipe calling for sugar. It's wonderful in coffee and tea too.

FOR "NO-FAIL" BRÛLÉE:

Rule 1: Never take your eyes off a brûlée. When heating the custard, watch for the liquid to reach its *first* undulation, then remove the pan from the stove. When broiling the crust, keep your eyes on the brown sugar; when it starts to bubble and caramelize (in about 5–7 seconds), quickly take it out of the oven.

Rule 2: The custard *must* be cold when you put it in the oven to create the crust. Four hours in the fridge is the minimum; overnight is better. If you are so inclined, partially fill a shallow roasting pan with chopped ice and put the ramekins on top, *then* put them under the broiler.

Rule 3: Brown sugar should be dry and clump-free. If yours isn't, sprinkle it on a paper towel and let it sit for an hour or so, then break it up into granules with your hands, or use a sifter.

Rule 4: Brûlée must be served immediately, or the crust will soften and you'll wind up with pudding.

Rule 5: The best chefs are well rehearsed. Try the recipe once before putting it on a party menu.

NOTE: "Granulated" brown sugar—sometimes called "brownulated"—is great for this recipe.

DO-AHEAD MISCELLANY

—Clean/soak the clams the morning of the party. Keep them refrigerated until ready to steam. You can make the "broth" for steaming the clams up to three days in advance, but allow it to come to room temperature before heating.

—If you purchase crabs live, you can prepare (i.e. kill) them early in the day; then keep refrigerated. NOTE: Ask your fishmonger for a mound of seaweed to cover the crabs (live ones or prepped) while they're in the fridge.

—You may prepare the carrot salad in the morning, but be advised: Curry (like soy sauce or salt) will grow stronger the longer it stands. Play it safe—add the curry about 15 minutes before serving.

—Corn bread is best hot from the oven, but if you must prepare it early, keep it sealed in a plastic bag *after it has cooled completely.* Before serving, remove it from the bag, wrap it in foil, and heat in a 325° oven for about 5 minutes or until hot.

—The custard for the creme brulee *should* be made in advance, at least 4 hours and up to 24 if you wish, so that it sets up properly.

NOTE: *The items on this menu do not freeze well.*

TRADE SECRETS FROM A THREE-STAR CHEF

15

What Do You Serve a Famous Chanteuse?

A THREE-STAR MEAT LOAF, THAT'S WHAT

Many people have influenced Anne's life and her cooking, but the most famous of them all—and her personal favorite—was Josephine Baker. If you were born around 1975, the year Ms. Baker died, you may never have heard of her, so allow us to provide a little background to set the stage.

Her fellow expatriate Ernest Hemingway said she was "the most sensational woman anybody ever saw. Or ever will." To the French, she was simply their beloved "La Ba-kair," the black American dancer and singer who tied a string of bananas around her waist and became one of the greatest entertainers of all time. And for those of you too young to know about the stir she created throughout the world in her heyday, let us take you back to 1925 to observe her electrifying opening night at the Theatre des Champs-Élysées*:

"She made her entry entirely nude except for a pink flamingo feather between her limbs; she was being carried upside down and doing the split on the shoulder of a black giant. Midstage he paused, and with his long fingers holding her basket-wise around the waist, swung her in a slow cartwheel to the

*From *Paris Was Yesterday*, by Janet Flanner, Viking Press, 1972.

Fresh Vegetable Tabouli

French Meat Loaf with Homemade Spiced Catsup à la Josephine

Pommes Frites

Chocolate Fudge Brownies

SERVES 4–6

stage floor, where she stood, like his magnificent discarded burden, in an instant of complete silence. She was an unforgettable female ebony statue. A scream of salutation spread through the theater.

"Whatever happened next was unimportant. The two specific elements had been established and were unforgettable—her magnificent dark body, a new model that to the French proved for the first time that black was beautiful, and the acute response of the white masculine public in the capital of hedonism of all Europe—Paris.

"Within a half hour of the final curtain on opening night, the news and meaning of her arrival had spread by the grapevine up to the cafés on the Champs-Elysées, where the witnesses of her triumph sat over their drinks excitedly repeating their report of what they had just seen....She was [to become] the established new American star for Europe."

Twenty-five years later, at the Roxy Theatre in New York City, Anne saw La Ba-kair in person for the first time. Through a twist of fate—and a bold dash toward her dressing room—she met her face to face after a performance. That chance encounter was the first of many that occurred during their twenty-year friendship, but that initial meeting was one of the most memorable. Anne recalls:

"I cannot tell you why she took a shine to me—perhaps she wanted to add me to her so-called "rainbow tribe" of a dozen young orphans of various nationalities, races, and religions. Was I her "Baker's Dozen"? I like to think so. She took me under her wing that night and invited me to join her entourage for dinner.

"The evening played out like soap opera. There were eight of us at the table and Josephine was the only black. When we were ready to place our orders, someone signaled the waiter, who came over with his pad and pencil at the ready. He went around the table and scribbled down all the appetizers, but when he returned to serve them, he forgot to bring Josephine's. Now, this may have been an oversight on his part, but we weren't there long enough to find out. All it took was the merest hint that she was being discriminated against—as she'd been in a famous incident at the Stork Club that same year—and she rose from the table, grabbed her coat, and fled.

"Naturally, everybody else got up and followed her out to the street, where we hopped into cabs and arrived at an apartment somewhere along Park Avenue. By now, everybody was famished, so the group decided to order sandwiches from a nearby deli. I almost fainted when I heard Josephine's order: what she wanted was a plain old meat loaf sandwich.

"When the food arrived, Josephine slipped into the kitchen and concocted a special sauce for her sandwich—a little tomato paste, some unlikely spices, a bit of orange juice. When I asked her what it was, she let me taste it and said with a giggle, 'It's catsup à la Josephine.' I thought it was delicious.

"I'll admit, this seems like quite an insignificant moment to remember. And I'm probably stretching things a bit too far to say the incident was sort of a culinary metaphor for her life. But as I look back on it now, what she did was really *so* like Jo Baker—she made something special out of nothing. She started out life as the daughter of a poor black servant in St. Louis and danced her way to a star-studded career the likes of which many celebrities today can only dream about. What other girl do you know who could put on a skirt of bananas and find such fame and fortune?

"She influenced my cooking in the same way she influenced me. I'm a Francophile because of her; certainly my love of French food should be apparent by now. But most of all, I learned from her that even the most mundane ingredients can be made unforgettable. All it takes is a flair for the dramatic, and knowing how to hold an audience."

Fresh Vegetable Tabouli

Because bulgur wheat is so filling, this dish, which originated in North Africa, could be a meal in itself.

1/3	cup extra-virgin olive oil
1/2	cup fresh lemon juice
1	cup medium cracked wheat (bulgur)
1	bunch scallions, finely chopped, including green part
1	large bunch curly parsley, coarsely chopped
4	large vine-ripened tomatoes, coarsely chopped
4	large stalks celery, coarsely chopped
1	large cucumber, peeled, deseeded, and coarsely chopped
1	large carrot, peeled and coarsely chopped
1	cup broccoli, coarsely chopped
	Celery salt, to taste
1/4	cup fresh mint leaves, finely chopped
Optional:	romaine leaves, for garnish

Mix the oil and lemon juice and pour it into a large (13 × 17) glass or ceramic casserole dish. Sprinkle the cracked wheat evenly over the liquid.

Layer the vegetables in the order given. Sprinkle all over with celery salt, then with the mint leaves.

Cover with plastic wrap and refrigerate for at least 24 hours.

To serve, toss all the vegetables, making sure the lemon and oil mixture thoroughly coats all the ingredients.

Serve chilled, on a romaine leaf or in a small bowl.

NOTE: *If you wish to serve the tabouli the same day you make it, pour the cracked wheat into 2 1/2 cups boiling water and simmer for about 30 minutes. Drain off any excess water, let sit until the wheat reaches room temperature, then fluff with a fork and add to the other ingredients. (Obviously, this variation does not require you to layer the vegetables.) Refrigerate the entire mixture for 30 minutes before serving.*

French Meat Loaf

With its French accent, this meat loaf qualifies as an entrée you'll be proud to serve to guests as well as family.

PREHEAT THE OVEN TO 350°.

1 1/2	pounds ground chuck
1 1/2	pounds ground turkey
2	eggs, mixed
1/2	cup dry bread crumbs
2	tablespoons sweet butter
1	medium onion, finely chopped
6	medium mushrooms, finely chopped
1/2	cup crushed tomatoes or homemade catsup (recipe follows)
1/2	tablespoon herbes de Provence
1	teaspoon salt
	Pepper, to taste
	Chopped parsley, for garnish

With a spatula or your hands, gently mix the chuck and the turkey with the raw eggs and bread crumbs. *Do not overmix.* Set aside.

Melt the butter in a sauté pan until bubbly. Add the onion and mushrooms and cook until soft. Reduce the heat to a simmer and add the tomatoes or catsup. Cook for five minutes, then remove from the heat and allow to cool. Add the *herbes de Provence,* salt, and pepper, and stir. Combine with the meat mixture. Again, *do not overmix.*

Place the meat loaf in an 8 1/2- to 9-inch loaf pan, and gently pat it into place. Put the loaf pan in a pan of hot water, making sure the water comes halfway up the sides of the meatloaf pan. Bake for one hour and ten minutes. Remove from the oven and let rest 10 minutes. Pour off the grease. To unmold, put a plate on top of the pan and carefully turn it upside down. Transfer the meatloaf to a platter, garnish the top with chopped parsley, surround it with pommes frites, and serve.

TEMPERATURE IS EVERYTHING...

...whether you're baking meatloaf or brownies. That's why good cooks never trust their oven dials. Case in point: A friend recently reported that his oven was overcooking, over-browning, sometimes burning his food, despite the care he took to set his oven dial to the required temperature. He called a repairman, who discovered the oven temperature was *75 degrees* hotter than it should have been. Even after being repaired, the stove still registered 25 degrees hotter, which the repairman noted was "actually pretty standard for your average oven." Solution: Always use a high-quality thermometer to measure oven temperature, then adjust up or down accordingly.

Also crucial: Find out your oven's quirks and requirements regarding the placement of shelves. Our friend discovered, after all these years, that he should have been baking in the lower third of his oven, not the middle, the location most people assume is the best for baking. Before another day passes, consult your owner's manual, or call the manufacturer.

Homemade Spiced Catsup
à la Josephine

You may want to double this recipe—it's delicious with luncheon meats, cold chicken, and of course, meat loaf sandwiches.

1/2	medium tomato, coarsely chopped
1	garlic clove, crushed
1	medium onion, finely chopped
One	6-ounce can of tomato paste
1/4	cup apple cider vinegar
3	tablespoons orange juice
2	teaspoons honey
1/2	teaspoon cayenne pepper
1/4	teaspoon cinnamon
2	tablespoons fresh basil, coarsely chopped
	Dash of nutmeg

In a medium-size bowl (not aluminum), mix all ingredients together until well blended. Do not refrigerate if you plan to serve this within 8 hours. To keep it for a week or two, pour the catsup into a glass jar with a tight-fitting lid and refrigerate. Bring to room temperature before serving.

TRADE SECRETS FROM A THREE-STAR CHEF

Pommes Frites

There's nothing so satisfying as classic French "fries" when they're properly made. The secret to success is double frying.

PREHEAT THE OVEN TO 300°.

4–6	Idaho or russet potatoes, peeled (or if you prefer, unpeeled and washed)
4–5	cups top-quality peanut oil

Using a mandoline, a food processor, or a sharp knife, cut the potatoes into long strips—either fat or thin, whichever you prefer. Set aside.

Into a *bassin à frites* (see box), pour the oil and heat it to 365°. Carefully add one handful of frites to the oil and fry for 2 minutes. (NOTE: They should *not* be browned.) Remove them to paper toweling and drain, then place in the oven to keep warm. Continue adding small batches—one handful at a time—and repeat the routine for draining until all the potatoes have had their first frying.

Recheck the temperature of the oil, making sure it is at 375°. One handful at a time, carefully refry batches of potatoes for a minute or so, until they are a honey brown. Remove and drain on toweling, and repeat the process until all the fries are done.

Serve immediately. Do not season the fries in any way—allow your guests to do it for themselves. Offer herb salt (see box, page 168) as an interesting alternative to regular salt.

MAKE YOUR OWN *BASSIN À FRITE*

If you're serious about your French fries, you can either purchase a French frying "basin," complete with a wire basket that fits into a ceramic pan—around $100 for the set—or you can make your own. Use a 2 1/2-quart, heavy ceramic casserole such as Le Creuset. Then insert a wire basket with a long handle (available at any housewares store and sometimes called a "French fry basket"). Make sure the basket clears the bottom of the casserole by at least 1/2 inch.

Buyer beware: Our experience with so-called automatic fryers (Fry-Daddy is one brand) has been negative. The oil never gets hot enough in these expensive gadgets, and cleanup is a nightmare.

TO MAKE HERB SALT

Add to a cup of coarse Kosher salt the following: 1 table-spoon each dried parsley, garlic powder, dried basil or thyme. For color, add 1/2 tablespoon paprika. For zip, add 1/2 table-spoon ground black pepper *or* 1 teaspoon white pepper.

Make your own concoction, using combinations of tarragon, curry, Parmesan cheese, marjoram, sage, ground fennel, dried mustard, sesame seeds, dried lemon peel, or dried orange peel.

Serve herb salt in special shakers, or in individual salt dishes.

Chocolate Fudge Brownies

These are rich and moist and delicious topped with whipped or ice cream.

PREHEAT THE OVEN TO 325°.

1/2	cup sweet butter
2	ounces unsweetened chocolate (use 1-ounce squares)
2	large eggs, at room temperature
1	cup "instant" or "superfine" sugar
2/3	cup flour
1	teaspoon real vanilla extract
1/3	cup dark chocolate chips
Optional:	1/2 cup nuts of your choice, coarsely chopped

Melt the butter and chocolate squares over medium-low heat (or microwave on medium power for 3 minutes); allow to cool slightly. With a whisk or an electric hand mixer, beat the eggs and sugar together until light and lemon-colored. Add the chocolate-butter mixture to the egg mixture and blend thoroughly, then add the flour, vanilla, chocolate chips (and nuts if desired).

Pour the batter into a well-greased 8-inch square cake pan and bake for 25 minutes. The brownies are done when a toothpick inserted in the center comes out almost, but not quite, clean. Cool on a rack, then slice with a sharp knife into 2-inch squares.

To serve, place a brownie on an individual plate that's been dressed up with a doily. Or place a dollop of whipped cream or ice cream on top.

FOR WORLD-CLASS BROWNIES

—Use the best chocolate you can afford. Some brands to keep in mind: Lindt Excellence, Callebaut, Guittard, Valrhona, Ghirardelli.
—For really moist brownies, remove them from the oven before they are completely done.

TIP: Soft crumbs will stick to a toothpick inserted into the center.

DO-AHEAD MISCELLANY

—This recipe for tabouli gets better with age. Make it up to a week in advance, but remember to drain off the excess juice if necessary.

—Combine the ingredients for the meatloaf in the morning if you wish; keep it covered in the refrigerator, but allow it to come to room temperature before baking. Spiced catsup can be made weeks in advance; keep it tightly covered in a jar in the refrigerator, but bring it to room temperature before serving.

—If you *must* slice your potatoes in advance, do so only 1 hour before you cook them. To prevent them from turning pinkish-brown, rinse them well and place them in an airtight plastic bag. Refrigerate.

—If you prepare the brownies in the morning or the day before, wrap each one individually in plastic wrap to keep them from drying out.

NOTE: *The items on this menu do not freeze well.*

16

Transforming the Ordinary

THE LITTLE TOUCHES MAKE *ALL* THE DIFFERENCE

During an entire week of dark and stormy weather a few summers ago—a period when few customers braved the elements to dine out on the East End—Anne spent her leisure hours critiquing various items that had been on the menu for a while and dreaming up ways to make them better. One dish under scrutiny was Herbed Snapper, scented with fennel and just a splash of Pernod. Garnished with parsley and long, graceful fennel fronds, it was a subtle creation that had gotten good response from customers. But since she'd made it so often, it became, to her, sort of boring to look at. How to transform it? She decided to add julienned carrots and a sprinkling of haricots verts for color and crunch. Then the stroke of genius: Why not cook and serve it en papillote—wrapped in parchment paper?

By the time the weather cleared, the newly transformed Herbed Snapper en Papillote was on the menu. Anne certainly expected it to move well on the evening of its debut, but she was really surprised when the waitress brought in an order for *four* snappers, all destined for the same table. Usually, when an entire group orders the same thing, it's either a signal word has gotten out that something is utterly spectacular and shouldn't be missed, or it's simply a sign that the guests are cowardly copycats. In this case, she knew it couldn't be the former since the dish was having its debut that very night. Convinced that this group fell into the latter category, she wanted to see what they looked like, and strode toward the dining room to take a peek.

There they sat, all of them quite nice-looking: well coifed, well groomed, well jeweled, very casual, the men with their sweaters draped Hampton-style about their shoulders, the women in their white slacks and silk shirts and shoulder-length hair cut just-so. They made quite a picture—a scene straight out of *Bonfire of the Vanities,* really. And when they looked up and saw Anne standing before them, she felt they must be thinking how sophisticated and smart they were—in fact, she nearly believed it herself, but the evening was still young.

"Ooooh, *en papillote*," they crooned in unison. Why, they were simply thrilled to see it on the menu, because the last time they'd had it was on their last trip to Europe, and they'd *loved* it.

When the snappers arrived at their table, the waitress opened each crisp, oven-browned package in succession. Then out billowed that steaming and wonderful scent filled with Pernod and vegetables and butter and fennel—the smell is just out of this world. And without a word, this chic foursome raised their forks, readied their palates, leaned in, and *ate the paper.*

Who would think that such a little touch—the parchment—could make such a difference. If you serve the Snapper in a well-lighted place, we're certain *your* guests will recognize a papillote when they see one. They'll also appreciate the way you've transformed the other, rather ordinary ingredients that make up this meal. Instead of taking the easy way out and serving, say, baked potatoes (aren't we all weary of them by now?), perform a little magic with your Cuisinart and produce the most delicate, crispy hash browns anyone has ever tasted. Then, rather than serving plain or buttered asparagus (wonderful, we admit), go the extra mile and toast some sesame seeds, chop some shallots, toss with a fruity olive oil and create an entirely new dish. As for dessert, who doesn't like fresh fruit? No one we know. But when you take green grapes and dress them up with sour cream and brown sugar, the combination of flavors and textures is a knockout.

Are these Herculean tasks? No. A bit labor-intensive? Yes, but only a bit. Worth the effort? There's only one way to find out...

Sesame Asparagus

This is a simple way to dress up asparagus. It's best when the asparagus are in season and just plucked from your garden, or when they're "flown in fresh" by your green grocer.

PREHEAT THE OVEN TO 500°.

2	*pounds asparagus, bottoms trimmed 1/2 inch*
1 1/2	*tablespoons extra-virgin olive oil*
2	*tablespoons shallots, minced*
2	*tablespoons sesame seeds, lightly toasted (see box)*
	Fresh lemon juice, to taste
	Salt, to taste

Fill a 12-inch sauté pan about 1/3 full of water and, in batches, blanch the asparagus until crisp-tender. Refresh them with cold water to stop the cooking, then drain and set aside.

Place the blanched asparagus in a shallow baking dish and toss them with the olive oil until well coated. Place in the preheated oven for 6 minutes; with a spatula or tongs, keep rolling the asparagus back and forth so all sides are heated. Sprinkle with the shallots and toasted sesame seeds and bake (and toss) one more minute. Just before serving, sprinkle them with a little lemon juice and a dash of salt. Serve immediately.

HOW TO TOAST A SESAME?

There are two ways:

—In a small sauté pan, toast the sesame seeds over medium heat while constantly shaking the pan. Watch carefully—sesame seeds toast quickly and can burn in a trice.
—Roast them on a baking sheet for 20 minutes in a preheated 350° oven. Shake occasionally so that the seeds brown evenly.

Never, never, never use oil when roasting sesame seeds—they've got plenty of their own! (Where do you think sesame oil comes from?)
See "Do-Ahead Miscellany" for tips about storing toasted sesame seeds.

Herbed Snapper en Papillote

Any firm-fleshed fish would be delicious in this recipe: snapper, salmon, black fish, flounder, cod, halibut, scrod. Choose firm vegetables: fennel, carrots, snow pea pods, haricots verts, scallions, baby peas.

PREHEAT THE OVEN TO 400°.

4–6	*sheets of parchment paper, cut into 8″ × 10″ sheets*
4–6	*snapper fillets, uniform in size and thickness*
1 1/2	*cups julienned vegetables (see headnote)*
4–6	*tablespoons Pernod or white wine or dry vermouth*
4–6	*tablespoons sweet butter, melted*
4–6	*tablespoons fresh herbs (if using dry herbs, use 4–6 teaspoons)*
	Salt and pepper, to taste

First, read "Parchment Primer," page 175, about creative options for folding parchment paper.

In assembly-line fashion, arrange the parchment papers in a row. Place one fillet on each paper, then add the following ingredients in order: a sprinkling of vegetables, the Pernod, the butter, a sprinkling of herbs, a dash of salt and pepper. Close up the parchment paper as you wish. Place the "packages" on a baking sheet and bake in the preheated oven for 7–10 minutes, depending on the thickness of your fillets. (The fillets will feel firm to the touch when done.) Serve immediately, and let your guests open the parchment themselves—it's a sensuous experience!

VARIATION 1: *Try substituting chicken fillets, pounded quite thin, and use the same ingredients as listed above.*

VARIATION 2: *For an Oriental flavor (to be used only with chicken), substitute 1 tablespoon each soy sauce, sesame oil, rice*

En Papillote

TRADE SECRETS FROM A THREE-STAR CHEF

wine vinegar or white wine for the Pernod and butter. In place of the herbs, use 1 teaspoon finely chopped ginger. Vegetables such as pea pods or snow peas work well in the Oriental mode, as does broccoli (which should be blanched first). Rice would be an excellent accompaniment to this variation. No need to alter the asparagus first course. Sorbet would be perfect for dessert.

PARCHMENT PRIMER

Experienced cooks know the value of parchment: use it as a liner and it will save every baking pan in your house; place it beneath the cover on a casserole dish to keep the moisture in; use it as a wrapping for fish or other quick-cooking items.

With a little practice, you can become an origami chef, using an 8 × 10 piece of parchment. For a simple presentation, place the fillet at an angle across the paper, then fold like an envelope to close, tucking the ends under. Or try a heart shape, folded in half, edges crimped. Use your imagination.

If, for presentation purposes, you want the parchment to turn a lovely golden brown, brush it with oil or melted butter before popping it in the oven. Left untouched, baked parchment becomes a light tan color.

Some brands of parchment recommend an oven temperature no higher than 400°. Check the label on your parchment box.

NOTE: *Never substitute paper grocery bags for parchment. They're apt to be unclean, full of chemicals, and may contain bugs!*

WHITE WINE WHINE

If ever there was a meal that cried out for white wine—a Vouvray would be perfect—this is it. A red wine, even a Beaujolais, would clash with the Pernod. NOTE: Don't even think about using a red wine *in* the dish itself: your fish fillets will turn pink, and so will the papillote.

Crispy Hash Brown Potatoes

There are three secrets to making really crisp hash browns: proper shredding of the potato, using a light touch while shaping, and keeping the oil hot enough. See box for tips about salting hash browns and other potato-based dishes.

4–6	*medium Idaho potatoes, peeled (or if you like a more hash brown, unpeeled and washed)*
1/2	*cup peanut oil*
Optional:	*1 cup finely chopped onion*
	Salt and pepper, to taste

Insert the medium shredding disk in your Cuisinart. Cut each potato lengthwise into fourths and follow the manufacturer's instructions for shredding. Process until all the potatoes have been shredded. If you're adding chopped onions, do so now.

NOTE: *After processing, cook the potatoes immediately or they will turn a dreadful pinkish-brown color.*

Pour the oil into a 12-inch sauté pan and heat on medium-high until bubbles form around the sides (or use the chopstick method of testing discussed on page 12). The temperature should be 365°.

With your fingers, gather up a scant cupful of potato shreds and carefully place them in the hot oil. With spatula, *gently pat down* to make a patty. Cook until the bottom is brown—about 3 minutes—then turn and cook about 2 more minutes. Remove and drain on paper toweling. Repeat until all the patties have been fried.

Serve immediately for crispiest potatoes, and let your guests salt and pepper to taste.

Green Grapes with Sour Cream and Brown Sugar

This is a classic example of transforming the ordinary. It's a dessert you'll want to serve again and again.

6–9	cups green grapes, washed and patted dry
1 1/2–2	cups sour cream
1/2–3/4	cup brown sugar

Place the grapes in a large bowl and add 1 cup of the sour cream. Mix together with your hands, then add more sour cream and mix again until the grapes are well coated but not overloaded with sour cream. (If the grapes are particularly large, you may have to use all the sour cream; if they're small, 1 1/2 cups should be enough.)

With a large spoon, scoop the coated grapes into individual bowls. Sprinkle each serving with a heaping tablespoonful of brown sugar. Serve immediately.

DO-AHEAD MISCELLANY

—The sesame seeds may be toasted well in advance; keep them in a cool, dry place, but never refrigerate! You may chop the shallots in the morning and keep them in a plastic bag until ready to use. Blanch the asparagus ahead of time, if you wish, but make sure to stop the cooking by refreshing it with cold water. Keep covered but at room temperature until ready to broil.

—Prepare the fillets, add all the ingredients, and wrap in parchment up to 2 hours in advance. Keep refrigerated, then allow them to stand at room temperature for at least 20 minutes before putting them in the oven.

—Remove the stems from the grapes early in the day if you wish. Keep the grapes refrigerated. Do not wash or dry them until you're ready to assemble the ingredients.

NOTE: *The items on this menu do not freeze well.*

17

A Guide to Handling the Persnickety Vegetarian

JUST FOLLOW THE GOLDEN RULE

We've always been disdainful of finicky eaters, hypochondriacs, food fetishists, and health freaks. They create problems for the cook, start fights with the guests, and simply take up valuable breathing room at a dinner party. But we do realize that the majority of people on this planet do not eat as we do. We know that three fourths of humanity has never tasted meat. We're aware that two thirds of the food consumed in the world is wheat, beans, corn, or rice. In much of Europe, South and Central America, Africa, and parts of Asia and the Middle East, beans and grains are the main sources of protein and carbohydrates. In Japan, sea vegetables such as kelp, dulse, and nori are so popular that the government grades them for quality, just as USDA grades our meat and dairy products. We're also aware that even here in North America—where 7 percent of the world's population still consumes 30 percent of the world's animal foods—there's a growing segment of the population trying to live a macrobiotic way of life.

Even so, we were quite taken aback when one of our regular catering customers from East Hampton called to announce she wanted a *totally vegetarian* meal for six prepared the following

Grilled Portobello
Mushrooms

Garden Fresh
Ratatouille

Homemade
Foccacia

Grand
Marnier–Glazed
Whole Oranges

SERVES 4–6

week. At first, we thought she was joking. Then we thought maybe she was just being stubborn and inflexible; certainly *some* of the guests could eat chicken or fish, couldn't they? As it turned out, what she wanted was precisely what she said she wanted: a totally vegetarian meal.

Panic set in, but not because we couldn't prepare a meal. Anyone could contrive to keep these creatures alive and nourished. The problem was, how to create a really interesting meal without the use of animal food: no meat, no chicken, no fish, no eggs, no milk, no butter.

After a week of experimentation with seaweed, tofu, and sprouts, we realized we were going about things in the wrong way. What we needed was a new attitude—and a fresh philosophy—about how to construct a vegetarian meal. We had to clarify our own values about food and look beyond our own eating habits. We had to reevaluate our thinking about what constitutes a "real" meal. What we discovered along the way are three principles—and one general rule—to keep in mind when preparing a vegetarian repast.

1. *A meal represents something more than food.* A meal is an act of sharing, at times a communion with another person. It feeds us physically, but it can also be a source of psychological comfort. The sight of a steaming bowl of homemade soup makes us feel cozy and protected from the ills of the world; a freshly baked loaf of bread soothes our New Age anxieties and returns us to earth. But a meal can send negative messages, too. The mess of a thrown-together casserole, the 90-second microwave TV dinner, the cheap bottle of wine served by someone who can afford better—all of these make us feel unloved, unimportant, unworthy. We should, therefore, strive for Principle 2:

2. *A meal should be tasty and visually appealing regardless of the type of food being served.* Of course we realize that, sometimes, one must acquire a taste for certain foods, be they animal or vegetable: shad roe, for example, is not everybody's immediate favorite, but then neither is

sauerkraut sushi or broiled tofu. Still, we believe any food can be prepared and served so that it is palatable. One who initially fears a pile of fish eggs might be cheered by the sight of a few pieces of crisp bacon tucked beneath. A first-time taster of tofu might be more quickly seduced by seeing it amid onions and carrots on a shish kebab, with a bowl of peanut sauce for dunking on the side. All of which segues into Principle 3:

3. *A meal should create a balance of textures and colors.* We've said it before: With the exception of ascetics and members of certain oddball religious sects who enjoy looking at the same gray gruel every day, most human beings prefer to have variety in a meal. The meat eater may want a whole steak for supper, but she'll also want some salad or a vegetable, and perhaps a light dessert to round things out. The vegetarian may crave a cheese-lentil loaf, but he'll look for millet and cooked greens as accompaniments, and maybe a sweet couscous cake to end the feast. Since we "eat with our eyes," keep color in mind as well. A meal composed of a beige piece of chicken, brown rice, and turnips will get lost on a plate; but sprinkle the rice with pimiento and substitute bright green beans for the turnips, and suddenly the meal comes alive.

The essence of these principles can be boiled down to one simple rule: *A meal should be fired by love and fueled with imagination.* With that in our hearts, we developed the following menu.

Grilled Portobello Mushrooms

When smoked on a grill, these taste almost "meaty."

PREHEAT THE BARBECUE GRILL (COALS SHOULD BE WHITE-HOT)
OR BROILER.

4	tablespoons extra-virgin olive oil
1	teaspoon dried thyme
4	large portobello mushrooms (roughly 4 inches in diameter), brushed to remove any dirt; stems removed
	Watercress, for garnish

Combine the oil and thyme and brush the mushrooms—top and bottom—lightly with the oil mixture.

Using tongs, place the mushrooms, tops down, on the grill for two minutes. Turn and grill the bottoms (the black part) for one minute. When the mushrooms are just barely starting to soften, remove them from the grill, slice into 1 inch wedges, and serve immediately, fanned out with a garnish of watercress.

If using a broiler, start with the tops up (nearest the flame) for a minute, then flip the mushrooms over so the bottoms are nearest the flame. Cook 30–45 seconds more.

Whatever method you use, *watch carefully* so that the mushrooms do not burn.

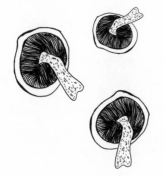

TRADE SECRETS FROM A THREE-STAR CHEF

Garden Fresh Ratatouille

This is a recipe to keep in mind when you're planning your spring vegetable garden.

PREHEAT THE OVEN TO 350°.

1	medium eggplant
1/4	cup cornstarch (for dredging the eggplant)
4	tablespoons extra-virgin olive oil
1	onion, coarsely chopped
1	clove garlic, smashed*
One	48-ounce can crushed tomatoes (not with puree added)
2	tablespoons sugar
2	teaspoons salt
1/2	teaspoon freshly ground black pepper
1	tablespoon fines herbes (see box, page 184)
2	zucchini, unpeeled, sliced into 1/2-inch rounds
2	yellow squash, unpeeled, sliced into 1/2-inch rounds
1/2	bunch basil, washed, stems removed, cut in a chiffonade (see box)
1/4	cup plain bread crumbs, preferably store-bought (or see box)
1	cup coarsely grated mozzarella cheese

Prepare the eggplant according to instructions (see box), then dredge it in cornstarch and sauté in 2 tablespoons of the oil until both sides are golden brown. Set it aside on paper toweling until cool, then cut it into 2-inch pieces.

(Continued)

*To smash a garlic clove, place it under the flattened side of a cleaver or chef's knife, then with your fist, firmly pound down. The papery hull will be easy to remove.

HOW TO PREPARE AN EGGPLANT

The excess moisture from an eggplant will ruin any recipe you put it in, so make sure you prep it first. Cut the eggplant horizontally into slices, rub the slices with lemon juice (to prevent discoloring), then salt both sides and place on several layers of paper towel to drain for about an hour.

THE CHIFFONNADE

To make a chiffonnade of basil (or other herbs and certain lettuces), arrange a stack of leaves (stems removed) then roll them into a cylinder. With sharp scissors (see box) or a knife, cut along the cylinder every 1/8 inch.

Heat the remaining 2 tablespoons of olive oil in a medium saucepan, on medium flame. Add the onion and cook until transparent. Add garlic and cook for an additional 30 seconds. Add the crushed tomatoes, sugar, salt, pepper, and *fines herbes*; mix well and simmer for 15 minutes. Remove from heat.

In a 9 × 15 casserole dish, layer the vegetables, adding sauce to the top of each layer, in the following order: zucchini at bottom, then squash, then eggplant on top. Sprinkle the basil over the eggplant. Pour the remaining tomato sauce over all. Sprinkle with bread crumbs, then grated cheese.

Bake in the preheated oven for 30–35 minutes, or until the cheese is bubbling and starts to brown.

HURRY-UP "HOMEMADE" BREAD CRUMBS

We've said elsewhere that storebought bread crumbs work fine with most recipes—and they're particularly good with the ratatouille here. But if you don't happen to have any and want to make your own in a hurry, try this: Put 2 pieces of dry toast in your Cuisinart and add a cupful of the following ingredients, alone or combined: low- or no-salt snack crackers, Zwieback, Melba toast, "common" crackers or oyster-type crackers, and unsalted pretzels. With the steel blade inserted, pulse until the mixture is in small crumbs.

This is a good recipe to keep in mind when you've got small amounts of stale crackers, etc. in your pantry that you can't bear to throw away. The bread crumbs keep for weeks in a tightly closed jar.

Homemade Foccacia

Not in the toniest restaurant in town, or the best bakery, will you find foccacia that can match this. Don't wimp out and buy one; make it yourself and blow your guests away!

PREHEAT THE OVEN TO 450°.

NOTE: *This recipe is designed for the Cuisinart only.*

1	cup warm water (90–100°—use a thermometer)
1/2	tablespoon dry barley malt or sugar
1	envelope active dry yeast (not the quick-rising type)
3	cups all-purpose flour, scooped and leveled, plus 1/2 additional if needed
1	tablespoon whole wheat flour
1 1/2	teaspoons salt
4	tablespoons extra-virgin olive oil
1/4	cup cornmeal
1	small onion, finely chopped
1/2	teaspoon dried sage
1/2	teaspoon dried rosemary
1/2	teaspoon dried basil
	Fresh ground pepper

Into a 2-cup glass measuring cup, pour the warm water, add the barley malt (or sugar), and stir until dissolved. Mix in the yeast and allow it to stand at room temperature until mixture begins to bubble—about 10 minutes.

Meanwhile, place the 3 cups all-purpose flour, the whole wheat flour, and the salt in the Cuisinart. Using the dough blade, pulse to blend.

(Continued)

Add 1 1/2 tablespoons of the oil to the yeast and water and mix well.

Start the Cuisinart and slowly add the liquid until a ball of dough forms and cleans the sides of the bowl. (See bread-making tips.) To finish the "kneading," keep the machine running for about one minute. (The ball will continue to rotate during this time.) Stop the machine and let the dough rest in the work bowl for about 10 minutes.

Remove the dough from the work bowl and shape it into a ball. Place the dough ball in a bowl with a little olive oil, turning it over until the entire ball is lightly oiled. Cover with plastic wrap and let the dough sit in a warm place until doubled in bulk—about a half hour. Then punch it down and allow it to rise a second time until doubled, roughly 20–30 minutes. Punch again, shape into a smooth ball, and set aside.

Sprinkle a 12-inch circular pizza pan or a 10 × 12 rectangular pan with the cornmeal. Place the dough in the center of the pan, and with a rolling pin or your hands, roll out the dough from the center in all directions to the edges of the pan. With your knuckles or fingertips, gently poke the dough so that slight indentations form.

While the dough is rising for a final time (about 15 minutes), combine the chopped onion, the remaining olive oil, and the herbs and pepper. With a pastry brush, gently apply the herb mixture to the foccacia, leaving the edges untouched. (If you wish, brush the edges with plain olive oil.)

Bake in the oven for 15–20 minutes, until golden brown. Remove and allow to cool. Serve at room temperature or heat for 5 minutes in a preheated (350°) oven.

BREAD-MAKING TIPS FOR NOVICES

If you've never made bread before, here are some basic tips that will help you achieve success:

1. Allow a full 10 minutes for the yeast to "prove" to you that it's working. If it doesn't bubble, throw it out and start over.
2. For this recipe, use the "scoop and level" method: With a 1-cup dry measure, scoop into your bag of flour so the measure is overflowing, then level it with the straight side of a knife. Don't pack the flour, and don't jiggle the cup in an attempt to "settle" the flour.
3. When bread is properly kneaded, it should look satiny or shiny. It will feel slightly tacky, but it will not stick to your hands. It should feel elastic.
4. Indoor temperature and humidity can affect dough. If your dough feels dry, spray it with water and pulse in your Cuisinart for a few seconds, then test it. If it's too wet, sprinkle with 1 tablespoon of flour, pulse, and test again.
5. Don't rush the rising; allow the dough to *double* in bulk each time.

NOTE: *Some breadmakers place a mark on the bowl to indicate where "doubling" will occur. For this recipe, 3 cups of unrisen dough equals 6 cups risen.*

6. If the dough "fights" you while you're trying to roll it out, slam it down on your work surface a few times, punch it, slam it down again, then let it rest for a few minutes.
7. If you like a crisp bottom crust, remove the foccacia from the oven when done, remove it from the pan, and place it on a rack in the oven. Turn off the oven and let the foccacia sit for about 10 minutes.

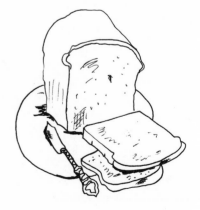

Grand Marnier–Glazed Whole Oranges

These beauties are sweet and succulent, yet free of fat.

4–6	seedless oranges
2	tablespoons Grand Marnier
	Water
1	cup apple, pear, or currant jelly
1/2	cup orange juice
1/4	cup orange juice concentrate
1 1/2	tablespoons cornstarch
3	tablespoons cold water

With a vegetable peeler or a very sharp paring knife, peel the outermost layer of one of the oranges (two if you're serving six people); slice this zest into thin strips and set it aside; remove the white pith. Peel the remaining oranges and remove the white pith.

Place the strips of orange zest in a small saucepan, pour in 1 tablespoon of the Grand Marnier, and add enough water to cover. Bring to a boil for a few seconds and then simmer for 8–10 minutes. Remove the strips from the pan and set aside.

Put the jelly, orange juice, concentrate, and the remaining Grand Marnier in a medium saucepan. Cook on medium-low and stir about 2–3 minutes, until well blended.

In a small bowl or measuring cup, add the cornstarch to the water and mix well. Add the cornstarch mixture to the orange mixture and cook on medium-low until it starts to thicken.

Carefully place the oranges in the saucepan and cook on medium-high for about 5 minutes, rotating the oranges and spooning the sauce over them all the while. Remove the saucepan from the heat and set it aside. (Do not remove the oranges from the pan.)

TRADE SECRETS FROM A THREE-STAR CHEF

To serve, scoop each orange onto a small serving plate or into a bowl, then drizzle sauce over the top. Garnish with the liqueur-flavored orange zest strips.

Serve warm and offer your guests a knife, fork, and spoon.

DO-AHEAD MISCELLANY

—The ratatouille can be assembled (except for the bread crumbs and cheese) a day ahead and refrigerated. Allow it to come to room temperature before baking.

—The foccacia is best when it's freshest—made the morning of your party—but you can get away with making it the day before if you allow it to cool completely, then store it in a large plastic bag tied with a twist tie. *Do not refrigerate.* Before serving, remove it from the bag and heat it in a preheated 350° oven for 5 minutes.

—You may prepare the glazed oranges up to 2 hours in advance. Keep them covered at room temperature. Warm over medium-low heat just before serving.

NOTE: *The items on this menu do not freeze well.*

18

You're on a Budget and the Queen Is Coming to Dinner

SERVE A FIVE-COURSE MEAL FOR UNDER $30

Back in the sixties, Anne had the good fortune to be invited to spend a month at a friend's villa on the island of St. Martin. Money was tight then and she knew she'd be living on a shoestring during those 30 days, but what did it matter? At daybreak, she lounged on the terrace of the villa, which stood at the highest point of the island and overlooked the turquoise waters of the Caribbean and the exquisite white beaches of Saba and Anguilla. In the afternoons, she watched the yachts glide around the harbor of Marigot, and picnicked on warm, sandy beaches nearby. At night, the entertainment was cooking for friends— perhaps a bit of freshly caught red snapper sautéed in butter, a jumble of fresh greens, a jug of red wine brought by a guest. Dinners weren't expensive because they couldn't be, but they were convivial affairs, delicious and memorable.

It was after just such an evening that Anne received a phone call. The voice on the other end was none other than that of her friend Blythe Carey,* the owner of the villa. She would arrive

*Names, and some details, have been changed. Discretion is as important in a chef as in a plastic surgeon.

Pumpkin Soup

Perfect Roast Chicken

Garlic Roasted Potatoes

Stir-fried Spinach

Hot Apple-Pecan Pie

SERVES 4–6

that evening to spend the night with Anne, and could they eat *in* rather than going out? And would it be an imposition to ask that Anne put her culinary skills to work for an additional four people? Of course, Anne agreed to the plan, but spent the next few hours in a panic, not because the meal preparation would be a challenge, but because Blythe Carey was who she was. More than that, Blythe might be bringing with her the infamous Earl of Wim! Before continuing with the story, a bit of background information is required. Anne explains:

"Blythe was a tiny Brit, but what an amazing powerhouse she was! When she was eighteen, she'd disguised herself as a man and actually fought during World War I—at least until she was discovered. Undaunted by that, she returned to the front as a surgical nurse. Later she took up taxidermy as a hobby, and apparently she spent a great deal of time going on safari to Africa and Asia and India.

"She was a woman of great wealth who traveled in the company of people like the Rockefellers. And she was outrageous in the best sense of the word: she kept a snake as a pet in her townhouse in London, and when she gave gifts to friends, she'd present them with things like *islands.* She was one of the most generous people I've ever known, but had a bizarre side to her, too.

"I discovered this at a dinner party she gave in her apartment in the south of France. She had spoken often of a dog—he was known as the Earl of Wim—and told me I would be meeting him that night. I was thrilled, because the gesture meant she considered me a close friend. I was also quite curious about this creature; when I asked people about him, they usually just smiled and said nothing.

"She ushered me into his room and directed me toward a diminutive figure resting on a velvet chaise longue. There lay the Earl of Wim—a stuffed Scottish terrier—amid some of his possessions: a genuine passport, a solid gold dogfood bowl and water dish, bones imported from India, a full-length sable wrap, a rhinestone cap, a pair of reading glasses, and his pet—a stuffed kitten. His royal dog house was situated on top of a nearby table; two cloisonné wolfhounds sat guarding the wrought-iron gate. I stammered hello and goodbye to the earl, and thanked Blythe for the introduction. What else could one say?"

That's enough flashback. We return to the problem: What sort of meal could be produced, on a budget, that would still be appropriate for the likes of Blythe Carey and her dapper dog?

"Despite what you might think, Blythe wasn't crazy, she was perfectly sane," notes Anne. "So I planned a meal of quite *normal* foods like roast chicken and spinach and potatoes and apple pie. In fact, I think the down-to-earth menu helped make the evening a great success. Blythe says the Earl is still talking about it."

To tally up the cost of this dinner party in today's prices, we recently spent an hour touring the aisles of King Kullen, one of the giant supermarkets popular here on the East Coast. note: We based everything on dinner for six. We also assumed that the cook would have a few of the basics on hand: sugar, salt, pepper, flour, olive oil, spices.

One 10-ounce can pumpkin	$.99
One 10-ounce can low-sodium chicken stock	.75
1 pint milk	.49
3 sticks butter	1.86
1 stick margarine	.43
2 lemons	.66
2 pounds spinach	3.58
8 large russet potatoes	1.29
3 cloves garlic	.39
1/2 pint heavy cream	.79
8 Granny Smith apples	2.99
1 cup pecans	3.34
Two 4-pound chickens	7.12
TOTAL:	$24.68

If you're used to eating store-bought croutons, you're in for a real treat when you make your own. They take only a few minutes—and you'll be amazed at how good they taste!

Simply slice 1-inch thick slices from a day-old baguette, then cut these into 1-inch cubes. Heat, on medium-high, 4 tablespoons extra-virgin olive oil until bubbly, then put the bread cubes into the pan. As soon as the bottoms of the croutons are browned (about 1 minute), turn them with a spatula and brown the other side. Remove from the pan and drain on paper toweling. Cool completely, then use as a garnish for soup or salad.

VARIATIONS: To make garlic croutons, add 2 teaspoons of minced garlic to the oil. For a bacon flavor, add 1 piece of bacon, coarsely chopped, to the oil. (Save the bacon bits to add to your salad.)

Pumpkin Soup

This beautiful soup would look great in small, scooped-out pumpkins, or in your favorite soup bowls. We like the crunch of croutons for garnish, but consult Chapter 5 for other ideas.

1	tablespoon sweet butter
1	tablespoon flour
2 1/2	cups chicken broth (plus another 1/2 cup if you like a soup)
1	cup milk
3	cups unflavored canned pumpkin
1	tablespoon brown sugar
1/4	teaspoon ground ginger
1/4	teaspoon kosher salt
1/8	teaspoon white pepper
	Homemade croutons (see box), for garnish

In a large sauté pan, melt the butter over a medium flame until bubbly. Whisk in the flour until well blended and cook for about 3–4 minutes. Slowly add 2 1/2–3 cups of the chicken broth, stirring constantly, then the milk. Add the canned pumpkin and continue to stir over medium heat. Add the remaining ingredients and stir to blend.

Serve immediately, with a few croutons floating on top.

NOTE: *Be patient. Allow the butter and flour mixture (a "roux") to cook for at least 3 minutes. Flour must be cooked thoroughly to lose its floury taste.*

Perfect Roast Chicken

The secret to this roast chicken is the 20-minute rotations. You'll never enjoy a more succulent bird than one prepared this way.

PREHEAT THE OVEN TO 425°.

2	chickens (3 pounds each for four guests; 4 pounds each for six)
1/2	cup extra-virgin olive oil
	Salt and pepper
2	lemons, halved
	Handful of herbes de Provence

Place each chicken on a rack in a roasting pan. Brush all over with olive oil and liberally salt and pepper each bird. Place 2 lemon halves and half a handful of herbs in each cavity.

Lay each bird on its side and roast for 20 minutes. Turn breast side up and roast for another 20 minutes. Turn on the other side and roast a final 20 minutes. Remove from the oven and allow to rest for 10 minutes.

To serve, place each chicken on a platter and surround it with Garlic Roasted Potatoes (recipe follows).

DON'T TOSS THAT CHICKEN CARCASS

Use it as the foundation of chicken stock. See page 24 for the stock recipe.

DRESS UP YOUR CHICKEN

If you want to jazz up the presentation of a whole roast chicken, try surrounding it with orange or lemon slices (or both), watercress, frizzled leeks (see Chapter 12), or tomato slices. When using sliced fruits or vegetables, try fanning them out, and "punctuating" every third or fourth slice with a bit of parsley or another herb.

If you prefer to serve chicken pieces and slices on a platter, set the carved chicken on a bed of lettuce. Try grouping legs and thighs together, fanned out on one side of the platter; then layer slices of white and dark meat on the other side.

—Don't salt potatoes before or during cooking. The salt draws out moisture that can cause a soggy result. Always taste first, then salt (just before serving in the case of potatoes).

—Are you aware of how many people salt (and pepper) food before they've even tasted it? All the more reason to ease up on seasoning food you're serving to guests. We like to gently remind our guests when a dish is "well seasoned"— they should actually try the food first, then decide on whether to use salt and/or pepper.

Garlic Roasted Potatoes

These potatoes are so rich, garlicky, and delicious, you may want to consider making more than you need—they're wonderful reheated the next day.

PREHEAT THE OVEN TO 350°.

1/4	*pound (1 stick) sweet butter*
6–8	*large russet or Idaho potatoes, peeled and sliced into thin rounds*
3	*cloves garlic, minced*
1	*cup heavy cream*
1/2	*cup milk*
	Salt and pepper

Using 2 tablespoons of the butter, grease a 12 × 15 inch casserole dish. Working quickly so they don't discolor, place the potatoes in the dish in overlapping layers. Cut the remaining butter into 1/2-inch chunks and sprinkle it over the potatoes. Combine the garlic, cream, and milk and pour over all. Sprinkle with pepper; do not salt until the potatoes are done.

Place the casserole dish in the preheated oven and bake for 45 minutes, or until bubbly and golden brown. Sprinkle with salt and serve immediately.

Stir-fried Spinach

This technique for preparing spinach surpasses any other we've ever tried.

4   tablespoons sweet butter

2   pounds fresh spinach, washed and dried, stems
      removed

      Freshly grated nutmeg

In a large (12-inch) sauté pan, heat the butter until sizzling. Stir-fry the spinach for about 45 seconds, stirring constantly, or until the spinach just begins to wither. Remove from the pan and serve immediately, with a sprinkling of nutmeg.

—Don't overwork pie crust dough or it will become tough.

—Roll the dough properly: Always begin in the center and roll away from you (rather than rolling back and forth and back and forth, which overworks the dough).

—Brush the top of a fruit pie crust with any of the following just before baking: cold milk, cold water, egg and cold water wash (1 egg to 1 cup water). Or sprinkle it with a little granulated sugar (white or brown) when it comes out of the oven.

—With cookie cutters or a kitchen knife, cut leftover dough into attractive shapes and place them on top of your crust. Then brush over all with cold water and bake.

Hot Apple-Pecan Pie

Have you ever known a guest who didn't swoon over home-made pie? This one is sweet and juicy, and the pecans add an unexpected crunch.

PREHEAT THE OVEN TO 425°.

	Pastry for a 2-crust pie (recipe follows)
6	cups tart apple slices, peeled, preferably Granny Smith
1	cup pecans, halved
1/2	cup sugar (or vanilla sugar, see page 157)
1/2	cup brown sugar, firmly packed
1	tablespoon flour
1 1/2	teaspoons grated lemon zest
1/2	teaspoon cinnamon
1/2	teaspoon cloves
1/2	teaspoon nutmeg
3	tablespoons sweet butter

Line the bottom of a 9-inch pie pan with 1/2 the pastry and set aside.

In a large bowl, combine the apple slices and pecans. Add the sugars, flour, lemon zest, and spices and mix together until blended.

Spoon the apple-pecan mixture into the pie pan and dot with the butter. Cover with the top crust (see box), make a few slits in the center of the crust to allow steam to escape, and bake in the preheated oven 40–45 minutes, or until the top is golden brown. Remove from the oven and cool on a rack for 10–15 minutes.

Serve immediately.

VARIATIONS: You may substitute walnuts or hazelnuts for the pecans. A handful of raw cranberries adds zing and color.

Pastry for a 2-crust pie:

2 3/4	*cups all-purpose flour*
1 1/8	*teaspoons kosher salt*
1	*stick sweet butter, chilled and cut into 1/2-inch chunks*
1	*stick margarine, chilled and cut into 1/2-inch chunks*
7	*tablespoons cold water, plus more if needed*

Combine the flour and salt in a Cuisinart work bowl by pulsing a few times with the dough blade. Add the butter and pulse 4–5 times. Add the margarine and pulse 4–5 times. The mixture should look like small peas. Add 7 tablespoons of water, then pulse a few times. Remove the work bowl cover and check the dough. It should stick together when you pinch it; if not, add another scant tablespoon of water and pulse again. (If making by hand, combine the flour and salt in a large bowl and mix well. Add the butter and margarine and work them into the flour with your fingertips or a pastry blender until the mixture resembles small peas. Add the water, a tablespoonful at a time, and blend with a fork. Gather up the dough into a ball.)

Transfer the dough to a lightly floured work surface. Gently knead about 10 times to distribute the butter, then shape into a ball and let rest for a few minutes. Cut the ball in half and flatten each half into a disk. Cover each disk with plastic wrap and refrigerate for at least 1 hour before using.

Roll out according to the instructions in the box.

DO-AHEAD MISCELLANY

—The pumpkin soup may be made a day or more in advance. Keep it covered in the refrigerator.

—Wash, dry, and stem the spinach early in the day.if you wish. Keep it refrigerated until ready to stir-fry.

—If you like serving chicken at room temperature, you can roast the chicken(s) in the morning. Allow them to cool completely, then cover them loosely with plastic wrap until ready to serve.

—The potato dish can be assembled in the morning as long as you add the milk mixture to keep it from drying out and discoloring. Keep it tightly covered with plastic wrap in the refrigerator.

—Your pie can be made the day before if you wish; before serving, heat it in a preheated 325° oven for about 10 minutes.

NOTE: *The items on this menu do not freeze well.*

TRADE SECRETS FROM A THREE-STAR CHEF

19

Faster Than a Speeding Chopstick

A STUNNINGLY SIMPLE BUT *FABULOUS* CHINESE MEAL

A fast Chinese meal? Sure, anybody can do that. But a Chinese meal that's fabulous? If you're *lucky,* you might find one in a restaurant near you. But if you're not, the best way to get authentic Chinese food is to cook it yourself—and this chapter will show you how.

Think back to the last time you ordered from your neighborhood take-out place—you know, the one that's wedged between the bowling alley and the pet store at the shopping center? Mmmm, so many of the house specialties sounded great. Number 5, Empress Chicken: tender morsels of succulent chicken enveloped in a delicate batter, deep fried and accompanied by a delightful special sauce with baby corn, bamboo shoots, and broccoli. Number 20, Pork Royale: shredded pork marinated in garlic and ginger, accented with fresh snow peas, and kissed with sesame sauce. So hard to choose, but you finally settled on Number 15, Ocean-Flavored Shrimp: giant shrimp stir-fried and served with shredded Chinese mushrooms, fresh snow peas, scallions, and peppers in a hot, spicy wine sauce. "It will knock you [sic] socks off," the menu vowed.

Promises, promises. Instead of a delicious mélange of ingredients, you got three big but tasteless shrimp floating in a dark brown, gelatinous sauce surrounded by a few mushroom stems, a handful of rubbery snow peas, and topped with slimy threads of scallions and dried pepper flakes. All of which you washed down with bitter green tea, followed by bright orange sherbet and a stale, uninspired fortune cookie that guaranteed your wisdom would bring contentment. Maybe not ordering take-out is the place to start.

But even at a formal, sit-down-style Chinese restaurant in a great metropolis like New York City, the dining experience is likely to be a disappointment. Not because the food is bad: It's the price that will make you feel queasy. A $30 entrée is not unheard of, nor is a $13 first course. Even desserts that don't belong on a Chinese menu—bananas flambé is a specialty at one midtown-Manhattan eatery—can cost nearly $10.

What can you do about it? Fight back by staying in! Why go out and pay top dollar for mediocre food when you can produce your own fantastic Chinese meal? In your own humble kitchen you can recreate the elements that once were the hallmarks of Chinese cuisine: a healthy blend of the freshest ingredients with delicate and subtle sauces; a balance of tastes and textures, of yin and yang; fine food, prepared from scratch, that's a delight to the eye and a joy to eat.

In the following pages, you'll find the secrets for making a no-fail Egg-Drop Soup and a quick and easy beef lo mein, plus some not-too-sweet recipes that may change the way you think about Chinese desserts. You'll also find suggestions for how to stock a Chinese pantry so that you are always prepared to whip up something delicious. But be forewarned: You may never want to leave home again.

TRADE SECRETS FROM A THREE-STAR CHEF

Egg-Drop Soup

Once you've made the Chinese chicken stock, you can assemble and serve this delicious soup in just five minutes.

6	cups homemade Chinese chicken stock (use recipe on page 111)
2–3	eggs, at room temperature, blended with a whisk
2	tablespoons dark soy sauce
2	bunches scallions, coarsely chopped
1	tablespoon sesame oil
Optional:	sprigs of cilantro, for garnish

Read "Egg-Drop Secrets" before proceeding.

In large saucepan, bring the chicken stock to a mad boil, then remove the pan from the stove. Immediately add the eggs, swirling them with a chopstick or a fork. Add the soy and scallions and swirl again. Allow the soup to rest for five minutes. *Do not reheat.*

Just before serving, add the sesame oil, a half-teaspoon at a time; taste and continue adding sesame oil to your liking.

Serve hot, in a large tureen, or in individual soup bowls. If you wish, garnish each serving with a sprig of cilantro.

NOTE: *If you wish to adjust the seasoning of this soup, use soy sauce. Do not add salt.*

EGG-DROP SECRETS

For perfect Egg-Drop Soup, follow these rules:

—Eggs should be at room temperature. (If you're ready to make the soup and have forgotten the room temperature rule, simply place the eggs in a bowl of warm [90°] water for two minutes, then proceed.)

—Blend, do not beat, the eggs; whisk to the count of 5.

—*Slowly* pour the blended eggs into the hot liquid (not in droplets but in a stream) and do so a few tablespoonsful at a time. Wait a few seconds between pourings—you want each portion to cook before adding the next, which will prevent an "explosion" of egg pieces in your soup.

—Use a chopstick or fork to swirl the eggs.

Stir-fry Beef Lo Mein

*We like to call this recipe "Beef and Whatever You Happen
to Have Around the House." But we've given you some direction
here, in case it's your first stir-fry.*

1	pound spaghetti, cooked al dente according to package directions
1/2	teaspoon sesame oil
1	tablespoon cornstarch
1	tablespoon Kikkoman soy sauce
1	tablespoon dry vermouth
2	tablespoons sugar
1	pound flank steak, cut across the grain into 1/8-inch strips
3	tablespoons peanut oil
1	onion, cut into 1-inch pieces
2	garlic cloves, crushed
3	cups fresh, firm vegetables, cut into 1-inch-long pieces 1/4 inch thick
3	tablespoons Heinz ketchup combined with 1 cup cold water
2	tablespoons oyster sauce

Toss the cooked spaghetti with the sesame oil and set aside.

In a small bowl, whisk together the cornstarch, soy, vermouth, and 1 teaspoon of the sugar. Add the meat and marinate
for at least 30 minutes. Do not refrigerate.

In a wok or sauté pan, heat 1 tablespoon of the peanut oil
until very hot and stir-fry the onion for 2 minutes, then remove
and set aside. Add the remaining 2 tablespoons oil to the wok,
heat on high flame, then add the garlic, the remaining sugar, and
the steak, and stir-fry until the meat loses its pinkness. Add the
vegetables and stir-fry for 1–2 minutes, or until the vegetables

are crisp-tender. Add the ketchup and water mixture, mix, and bring to a boil. Add the onions and oyster sauce and mix well.

Pour over the cooked spaghetti and toss to coat. Serve immediately.

VARIATION: *Instead of flank steak, substitute chicken or shrimp. This recipe can be completely vegetarian, too: just substitute additional vegetables for the meat.*

DO-AHEAD CHINESE "SPAGHETTI"

If you've ever had a meal at a "pasta palace"—where hundreds of people are served myriad varieties of pasta every night—you may have wondered, How do they do it? Answer: Much of the pasta is precooked in the morning and reheated, briefly, in boiling water. When time is of the essence, you can do this, too, on a smaller scale.

For Chinese spaghetti, follow the pasta package instructions for "al dente," then remove it from the water and put it into a large bowl. Mix in 1/2 teaspoon sesame oil to keep the pasta from sticking and set aside. Just before serving, plunge the pasta (held in a colander) into boiling water for 20 seconds, then drain and serve.

—Slice and deep-fry as noodles to use for snacks or as the crunchy foundation for "chow mein" or other stir-fry recipes.
—Shape into raviolis and stuff with julienned vegetables or ground meats, then fry into wontons.
—Make raviolis as above, but poach in stock or soup for dumplings.

TIP: Always seal wontons with an egg wash. (See Chapter 10 for more information about the world of wontons.)

THE EVER-READY CHINESE PANTRY

When you get the urge for Chinese, do you dial c-a-r-y-o-u-t? No need to, if you've got these basics in your pantry. Add some fresh vegetables, some meat or fish, and a bit of imagination.

sesame oil
soy sauce
ginger
garlic
peanut butter (for Peking noodles)
linguine or spaghetti
long grain rice
chili paste (for Szechuan or "hot" flavor)
hoisin sauce (similar to oyster sauce but stays fresh longer)
cornstarch (for thickening sauces)
chicken stock (homemade, or low-sodium canned will do)
peanut oil for frying
sliced water chestnuts, canned (if you can't get fresh)
bamboo shoots, canned (if you can't get fresh)
Optional but incredibly versatile: egg roll wrappers (see note)

TRADE SECRETS FROM A THREE-STAR CHEF

Sweet-Sour Lemon Ice

You've never gotten this at a Chinese take-out place.

5	cups water
2	cups sugar
1 1/3	cups fresh lemon juice
2	tablespoons grated lemon zest
Optional:	mint leaves, for garnish

In a medium saucepan, combine the water and sugar and stir until the sugar is nearly dissolved. Heat over medium-high flame until the mixture boils and cook, uncovered, for about 5 minutes. Do not stir.

Pour the liquid into a ceramic bowl and refrigerate for at least 1 1/2 hours. Then add the lemon juice and zest and stir to blend. Pour the mixture into an ice cream machine and follow the manufacturer's instructions. If you don't have one, see page 36.

To serve, spoon into individual bowls and, if you like, garnish with mint leaves.

Almond Crescents

We hope these will replace the ubiquitous fortune cookie.

PREHEAT THE OVEN TO 425°.

2	*sticks sweet butter*
1/2	*cup sugar*
2 1/2	*cups flour*
2	*tablespoons brandy or rum*
1/2	*cup finely ground almonds*
	Confectioner's sugar, for dusting

Cream the butter and sugar until fluffy. Add the flour, brandy, and almonds and mix together using an electric hand mixer.

Place the dough on a lightly floured board and roll out to about 1/4 inch thick. Cut out crescent shapes with a cookie cutter.*

Place the crescents on an ungreased cookie sheet and bake in the preheated oven for 10 minutes, or until lightly browned. Sprinkle with confectioner's sugar while still warm.

Serve at room temperature.

VARIATION: If you don't happen to have almonds for this recipe, you can substitute 1/2 cup walnuts or pecans or hazelnuts, or a combination of these.

*If you don't have a crescent-shaped cutter, use a round cutter or an inverted glass. With a sharp knife, slice the rounds in half, then "bend" them into crescent shape with your fingers.

TRADE SECRETS FROM A THREE-STAR CHEF

DO-AHEAD MISCELLANY

—You may assemble the soup (except for the eggs) in the morning. Do not refrigerate.

—To speed up the stir-fry, you may cut up all the vegetables, mix the sauce, even cook your spaghetti (see box) in the morning. Keep the vegetables covered but at room temperature.

—You may prepare the lemon ice well in advance, but allow it to stand at room temperature for 15 minutes so it's easier to spoon into serving dishes.

—The almond crescents are best fresh, but you can make them the day before. Allow them to cool completely, defer the dusting of confectioner's sugar until later, then place the cookies in a plastic bag and keep them at room temperature. Before serving, reheat for 5 minutes in a pre-heated 300° oven, then dust with sugar.

NOTE: *Except for the lemon ice, the items on this menu do not freeze well.*

Liberté, Egalité, Fraternité!

AT LAST! A MEAL THAT SUITS THE *COOK'S* SCHEDULE

*J*ust because a person loves to cook, it doesn't mean she (or he) wants to become a martyr. But the more one becomes the master of one's kitchen, the more an insidious attitude creeps over one's family and friends. "Oh, don't worry about old Jane—she's never happier than when she's making a meal"—no matter that it's 110° in the kitchen and everyone else is out on the breeze-swept deck sipping gin and tonics.

This patronizing attitude can get completely out of hand among spouses and Significant Others, who often assume the uninvited role of food critic. Offered an experimental dish of, shall we say *omelette à la Reine,* he—and no one but a *he* would dream of being so insensitive—will masticate thoughtfully for a moment and then opine, "Not bad, but the chicken is a bit over-done and the egg mixture could use a trifle more browning." If the chef objects, her spouse will adopt a hurt expression and protest, "But you *asked* me to tell you what I thought."

Then there is the familiar assumption that if a restaurant can produce any given meal on 20 minutes' notice, a hostess should be able to do so just as easily. You're probably familiar with the scenario: Your SO is bringing out guests from the city on Friday afternoon, and you've timed everything down to the minute—

Radis au Beurre

French Lasagne with Bechamel Sauce

Tossed Green Salad

Mocha-Walnut Torte

SERVES 4–6

your homemade soup is bubbling away, the popovers are at T minus 30 and counting, and your roast is just about ready to come out of the oven for a brief respite. The vegetables have been blanched and refreshed, and the ingredients for your soufflé are on standby. Then you get the call: "Jack-knifed tractor-trailer. Oil spilled all over the freeway. We're looking at another hour or so, honey. Hold dinner for us?" You hang up the phone, mix a bone-dry martini, and watch your billowy popovers—and the evening—shrivel and collapse before your eyes.

So let's take a moment right here and now to outline a Declaration of the Rights of Cooks:

1. Every dinner should be what the cook feels like cooking that day.

2. Every dinner should taste good, but that doesn't mean it has to be a gourmet extravaganza.

3. When the guests are family, preparation and cleanup should be an exercise in participatory democracy.

4. If food is love, the cook is the one who should be loved the most.

Now, how to attain such nirvana? Don't make reservations; instead, design a meal that's virtually goof-proof, one that can go with the flow (and we don't mean via the current from your microwave). Start by selecting recipes that can be prepared the morning of your party or, better yet, the day before. Choose foods that "hold" well, such as a stew that can simmer indefinitely. Side dishes that can be held in a *bain-marie* can save the day, as can salads, or vegetables that require only last-minute steaming and blanching. Be flexible—choose entrées and side dishes that can expand with the crowd. If a surprise guest shows up, you're ready.

Of course, many meals could fit this category—a pot of chili, almost any casserole, or a vat of Sloppy Joes, for example. They're fine in their place, but we prefer a meal that says understated elegance. So we've started ours with Radis au Beurre (translation: "Radishes with Butter"), an appetizer that can be prepared in two minutes, sit for hours in the refrigerator, and not show it. And while guests are seething on the Long Island

Expressway, Anne's French Lasagne (made 24 hours earlier and unlike any lasagne you've ever tasted) will wait to be popped into the oven. Of course, you know the virtues of a tossed salad—torn into bits and spun in the morning, it's in no hurry to be dressed. The happy ending: a walnut torte (made the night before) that really gets better with age.

Radis au Beurre

Unless your guests are familiar with French appetizers, they probably won't ever have eaten this classic. It's an unusual but delicious way to start a meal.

6	radishes per person, preferably the long type, washed, dried, and ends trimmed
2–3	sticks sweet butter or Herb Butter (see box), at room temperature
1	loaf cocktail-size pumpernickel or black bread
	Salt
	Freshly ground pepper

The object here is for guests to make their own little sand-wiches.

Just before serving, slice the radishes either into rounds or oblongs about 1/4 inch thick, and fan them out on salad plates. Place 4 tablespoons of butter per person into individual ramekins, or arrange it attractively on the plate with the radish-es. Serve the bread either on a platter or on individual plates, and keep salt and pepper within reach.

French Lasagne with Bechamel Sauce

This lasagne is subtle, elegant, and has nothing in common with the stuff you ate after the football game when you were a teenager.

PREHEAT THE OVEN TO 350°.

4	*tablespoons sweet butter*
1/4	*cup coarsely chopped boiled ham*
1	*cup coarsely chopped onions*
1/2	*cup coarsely chopped carrots*
1/2	*cup coarsely chopped celery*
2	*tablespoons olive oil*
1	*pound ground chuck (see box)*
1/2	*cup dry vermouth*
2	*cups beef stock*
One	*6-ounce can tomato paste*
2	*tablespoons flour*
1	*cup milk*
	Dash of freshly ground nutmeg
1	*pound lasagne noodles (cook "al dente" according to directions)*
1/4	*cup freshly grated Romano cheese*
	Salt and pepper

Melt 2 tablespoons of the butter over moderate heat and add ham, onions, carrots, and celery and cook, stirring, for about 10 minutes. (See box about Mirepoix.) Transfer to a saucepan.

Heat the olive oil in the same sauté pan and lightly brown the meat, breaking up any lumps. Pour in the vermouth and boil

(Continued)

BEST BLEND FOR GROUND CHUCK

When making lasagne, ask your butcher for an "80-20 blend" of ground chuck. That's a mixture of 80% lean plus 20% fat...just enough lean to be healthy, just enough fat to be flavorful.

DIETER'S NOTE: Instead of ordering ground beef labeled "lean"—it has no fat and there-fore no taste and cooks up dry and is simply awful—substi-tute ground turkey. It's low in fat and has a little moisture and flavor.

THE BEST BECHAMEL

You may have read in other cookbooks that hot or scalded milk is the key to a smooth, lump-free bechamel. Not true! Cold milk, added slowly while you whisk the flour mixture, works best and results in a better-tasting white sauce. There's no floury aftertaste whatsoever!

What makes a lasagne French? More than the bechamel sauce, it's the mirepoix, a mixture of chopped onions, carrots, celery, and ham (or another pork product) that has been "sweated" in butter. It's a great flavor enhancer that you can add to almost any recipe calling for ground meat. Also superb with shellfish. Or mix it into bechamel or white sauce, or savory gravies for poultry or pot roasts.

How to make a French pizza: Just spoon a cupful of mirepoix over the crust, then follow with tomato sauce and your favorite ingredients.

until the liquid almost evaporates. Add the meat to the saucepan and stir in the stock and tomato paste. Bring to a boil over high heat. Then reduce the heat and simmer the sauce, partially covered, for 45 minutes.

Meanwhile, make the bechamel sauce by heating the remaining 2 tablespoons of butter in a clean sauté pan. When bubbly, whisk in the flour until thoroughly blended. Cook over low heat for 3 or 4 minutes, then slowly add the milk. Continue to whisk the mixture until it thickens. Add the nutmeg and stir. Remove from the heat and set aside.

Into a 9 × 15 lasagne pan, pour a thin layer of meat sauce. Then layer remaining ingredients—noodles, then sauce, then bechamel, noodles, sauce, bechamel, etc.—until the pan is nearly full and the final layer is bechamel. Sprinkle with the Romano and a little salt and pepper.

Place the pan in the preheated oven and bake for 25–30 minutes, or until bubbly. Remove from the oven and let rest for 10 minutes.

To serve, slice into squares and place on individual dinner plates. Serve with crisp baguettes and salad (recipe follows).

VARIATIONS: Try combining ground veal or ground pork with the chuck—a 50-50 blend.

If you want to serve a vegetarian lasagne, simply substitute 4 cups of firm vegetables for the meat. Or try substituting 5 cups of mushrooms—a blend of shitakes, oysters, and whites is great.

NOTE: Avoid portobellos in this recipe, since they will blacken your bechamel sauce.

Tossed Green Salad

This salad is designed to be a subtle accompaniment to the French Lasagne. Don't be tempted to add more vinegar or oil than the recipe calls for or the salad will overpower the main course.

2	tablespoons balsamic vinegar
4	tablespoons extra-virgin olive oil
4–6	cups mixed greens (see box)

Just before serving, whisk the vinegar and oil to emulsify. Then add one tablespoon at a time to your salad, and toss gently with your hands. When the greens are just barely coated, stop adding dressing. Serve immediately.

IMPORTANT WINE TIP: Never serve wine—red or white—with a salad course that contains vinegar. The combined level of acidity will destroy the taste of the wine and *the salad. If you must serve a beverage during the salad course, try mineral water, plain or fizzy.*

NOTE: This double-acid problem does not occur if you serve the salad with *your entrée or another dish. Your taste buds will be kept too busy to notice.*

MIXED GREENS

Here are just some of the greens you can toss for a mixed green salad: romaine, arugula, Belgian endive, curly endive (a.k.a. chicory), green or red leaf lettuce, radicchio, watercress, spinach, Boston or Bibb lettuce, collard greens, fennel, and celery ribs.

NOTE: Although most of these greens can stand alone, curly endive by itself can be overpowering—too bitter! Experiment with different combinations and remember that your choice of dressing can dramatically alter the flavor of any salad.

RIP TORN AND OTHER SALAD TIPS

Never cut lettuce or other salad greens with a knife; you'll bruise the greens, and the cut edges will turn dark. Just rip or tear the greens into bite-size pieces.

One kitchen "gadget" you shouldn't be without: the homely—but highly effective—salad spinner. Absolutely the best way to remove water from lettuce or other greens. The machine does all the work, and the lettuce stays crisp and fresh. For roughly $20, this is a good investment!

Mocha-Walnut Torte

This luscious dessert is light and rich at the same time. Serve it with steaming mugs of unsweetened coffee or cappuccino.

PREHEAT THE OVEN TO 350°.

2 3/4	cups walnuts plus 3/4 cup for topping
1	teaspoon espresso powder
1/2	teaspoon cocoa powder
1/2	cup cake flour
1	cup sugar (or vanilla sugar, see page 157)
6	eggs, separated
1	teaspoon grated lemon zest
1	teaspoon freshly ground nutmeg
1	teaspoon brandy or rum

Grease two 8-inch round cake pans and line them with parchment or waxed paper. Grease the paper liners.

Using the steel blade of your Cuisinart, process the walnuts to a fine grate and remove 3/4 cup for later use. Add the espresso, cocoa, and flour to the work bowl and pulse until the ingredients are well mixed. Pour the mixture into a large bowl and set aside.

Into a small bowl, pour half the sugar, the egg yolks, and the lemon zest and beat with an electric mixer until thick, about 2–3 minutes. Add the nutmeg and liquor and continue to beat until blended.

In a separate bowl, beat the egg whites until foamy. Then add the remaining sugar, a tablespoon at a time, and continue beating until soft peaks form. Into this mixture, pour the egg-lemon sauce and fold the two mixtures together with a spatula.

Continuing with the spatula, gently fold in the grated nuts, about a half-cup at a time, until just blended.

Pour the batter into the prepared pans and bake for 25–30

minutes, until a toothpick inserted in the center comes out clean. Allow the layers to cool in the pans, then turn out onto individual plates.

For the frosting:

4	*ounces sweet chocolate*
1	*tablespoon espresso powder*
2	*tablespoons hot water*
3/4	*cup sweet butter*
1/2	*cup confectioner's sugar*

In a microwave, melt the chocolate on 50% power for 3 minutes (or use a double boiler). Add the espresso and water and stir until blended. Remove from the heat and allow to cool.

Cream the butter with an electric mixer or by hand. Add the chocolate mixture and confectioner's sugar and beat until smooth.

Spread a layer of frosting between the cake layers, then frost the top and sides. Sprinkle the top and sides with the reserved grated walnuts.

VARIATION: If you want to lighten up this dessert, you may substitute whipped cream (sweetened ever-so-slightly) for the frosting. No need to frost the sides; just spread the cream over the center and over the top. Sprinkle with grated nuts.

DO-AHEAD MISCELLANY

—You may wash and trim the radishes early in the day, but don't slice them until just before serving or they'll dry out. Rinse in cold water and keep in a plastic bag until ready to slice.

—The flavor and texture of the lasagne improves if assembled a day in advance. Keep it loosely covered with plastic wrap in the refrigerator, but bring it to room temperature before baking.

—Any lettuce salad can be rinsed and torn in advance. After spinning in a salad spinner to eliminate most (but not all) of the water, refrigerate until ready to use. The dressing may be made days in advance and kept in the fridge.

—The torte holds up well if baked a day in advance. Make sure the cake is absolutely cool before you slip it into a plastic bag. Do not refrigerate. Do not make the frosting or frost the cake more than 1 hour in advance. (A whipped cream frosting should be whipped and applied to the cake just *moments* before serving.)

NOTE: *The items on this menu do not freeze well.*

Index

freezing, 92

Mushrooms
  and broccoli omelette, 34–35
  grilled portobello, 182
  as substitute for meat, 216

Mussels
  eating, 138
  overcooking, 138
  refrigerating, 145

Mussels Mandarin, 138

Mustard-honey glaze, with
    salmon fillets, 42–43, 48

National Pork Producers'
    Council, 139

Navarin Printaniere, 19

Navarin of Shank of Lamb with
    Spring Vegetables, 17, 19,
    20–21, 26

Noodles, 206
  Peking scallion, 105, 112

Nylon bristle brush, 86, 123

Ocean-Flavored Shrimp, 201–2

Oil
  cooking, 11
  frying
    for leeks, frizzled, 131
    for rice, 109
    for shrimp wontons, 117
  olive, 11, 63, 82, 152, 194,
    217
  peanut, 152
  sesame, 173
  vegetable, 152

Okra, in shrimp gumbo, 148

Olive oil, 152
  in Artichokes Hollandaise, 82
  in Breast of Chicken Olivado,
    11

and croutons, 194
  in Good-for-You Potato
    Skins, 63
  in Tossed Green Salad,
    217

Omelette
  broccoli and mushroom,
    34–35
  Madame Poullard's Omelette,
    34–35
  pan for, 35

Omelette à la Reine, 211

Onions
  balsamic, and calve's liver, 72,
    77
  chopping, 32
  dehydrated, 61
  sautéing, 77
  See also Vidalia onions

Orange Almond Salad, 142

Oranges, 145
  Grand Marnier-glazed whole,
    188–89
  Valencia vs. "blood," 142

Oriental food, 116, 174–75
  See also Chinese food

Orzo and Pepper Casserole, 143,
    145

Ossobucco, 17, 22–23, 26

Oven, temperature of, 165

Oven-Braised Brisket of Beef,
    59, 60, 61–62, 67

"Paillard of Veal," 11

Pan
  for crepes, 123
  for omelettes, 35
  See also Sauté pan

Paper grocery bags, 175

Parchment paper, in Herbed